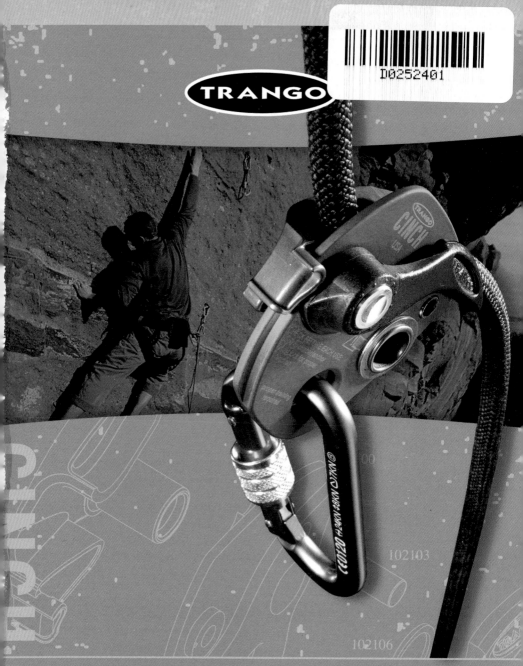

TRANGO

D0252401

LOAD

BELAY

LOCK OFF

LOWER/RAPPEL

The Cinch is the next generation belay device.
Feeds rope fast, provides bomb-proof lock-off
and predictable lowering. Designed for sport
climbing and top-roping with a single rope.
Rope Diameter: 9.4-11mm

www.trango.com   800.860.3653   Boulder, Colorado USA

WARNING:

Rock climbing is a sport with inherent danger, which may result in severe injury or death. Read and understand this warning before using this book. This book is not intended to serve as an instructional manual and should not take the place of proper instruction. Employ a professional guide or instructor if you are unsure of your ability to handle any circumstances that may arise. The information contained within this book is a compilation of opinions and as such, is unverified. These opinions are neither facts nor promises and should not be treated as so. Rely first and foremost upon your skill, experience, conditions, and common sense rather than the opinions expressed in this book including descriptions, safety ratings and difficulty ratings, as they are all entirely subjective. If you are unwilling to assume complete responsibility for your safety, and if you (or your estate) is unwilling to never try to sue Fixed Pin Publishing if you get hurt or killed, do not use this guidebook.

Errors may exist in this book as a result of the author and/or the people with whom they consulted. Because the information was gathered from a multitude of sources, they may not have been independently verified and therefore **the publisher, or the authors, cannot guarantee the correctness of any of the information contained within this guidebook.** In addition, information suggesting the safety of a route, its difficulty, or equipment used may be incorrect or misleading. Fixed protection may be absent, unreliable, or misplaced.

THE AUTHORS AND PUBLISHER EXPRESSLY DISCLAIM ANY REPRESENTATIONS AND WARRANTIES REGARDING THIS GUIDE. THEY MAKE NO REPRESENTATIONS OR WARRANTIES, EXPRESSED OR IMPLIED, OF ANY KIND REGARDING THE ACCURACY OR RELIABILITY OF THE CONTENT OF THIS BOOK. THERE ARE NO WARRANTIES OF MERCHANTABILITY OR FITNESS FOR A PARTICULAR PUPROSE. THE USER ASSUMES ALL RISK ASSOCIATED WITH THE USE OF THIS BOOK AND ALL ACTIVITIES CONTAINED WITHIN IT, ESPECIALLY ROCK CLIMBING.

North Table Mountain: Rock Climbs at the Golden Cliffs

Authors: Jason Haas and Ben Schneider
Action Photographs: Ben Schneider and Jason Haas, unless otherwise credited.
Description Photographs: Jason Haas

© 2008 Fixed Pin Publishing, LLC
All rights reserved. No part of this book may be used or reproduced in any manner without written permission from the publisher.

Cover Photo: Norie Kizaki on *The Perfect Ten* 5.10a, by Ben Schneider

ISBN 978-0-9819016-0-2
Library of Congress Control Number: 2008908963
Printed in the United States

Fixed Pin Publishing is continually expanding its guidebooks and loves to hear from locals about their home areas. If you have an idea for a book or a manuscript for a guide, or would like to find out more about our company, contact:

Ben Schneider
Fixed Pin Publishing
P.O. Box 3481
Boulder, CO 80307
ben@fixedpin.com

Jason Haas
Fixed Pin Publishing
P.O. Box 3481
Boulder, CO 80307
jason@fixedpin.com

NORTH TABLE MOUNTAIN
Rock Climbs at the Golden Cliffs

Jason Haas
Ben Schneider

Dave Kelly, *This Ain't Naturita Pilgrim* (5.9), p.87

Dedication

Jason -

To my dad Bruce, for giving me that spunk to get after it.

Ben -

To my parents, for raising me, putting up with me, teaching me to be a good man, and trusting that I wouldn't kill myself when I started down this path.

Acknowledgements

We owe a tremendous thank you to several climbing partners in particular, including Brian Young, Tony Bubb, Geoff Elson and Sam Shannon. Richard Berk gave us a copy of his old guide *Welcome to Walk* and wrote a terrific historical essay on the area. Justin "Judd" Salvas was an incredible resource, donating hours of his time and expertise. Gary Landeck at the American Alpine Club Library provided invaluable support during the research phase of the book and heartfelt appreciation goes out to Rob Kelman for helping with the technical aspects of book production. We would like to thank Peter Hubbel and Mark Rolofson for paving the way with their old books. Also, Ken Trout for his Rock and Ice article as well as his selfless act of replacing countless unsafe bolts and anchors. Our photography models gave us many hours of their time, repeating pitches countless times until they learned how to be a good model (or the photographer learned what an f-stop was): Laramie Duncan, Norie Kizaki, Jon Haradon, Christine Hill, and Adam Stack. The staff of Neptune Mountaineering went above and beyond in their efforts to educate us about the industry. The authors would like to thank Dave Wolf for generously sharing his business savy. Jason also wants to extend his gratitude towards Jerry Carmody for his behind the scenes work. Without him, he would not have been involved in this project. Others that deserve recognition include Lee Landkamer, Carrie Hoelsi, Kate Carmody, Jose Yavari, Wayne Crill, Richard Wright, Stacey Sagesse, Chris "The Mountaineer" Donharl, Dan Hare, Deaun Schovajsa, and Kirk Miller. Also, thanks to Kate Calder, Ryan Kane and Scott Borger for donating photos.

Jason Haas, *Rafiki* (5.12c), p. 100

photo: Tony Bubb

Preface

It has been an unusual winter; one characterized with more snow and colder temperatures than in most years. Cabin fever has set in and all the mortar around my doorframes has begun to loosen from too many pull ups. The local gym scene has stagnated and motivation wanes as I move from the blue route to the green route. Ben Schneider and I decide to brave a day at the Golden Cliffs, historically referred to as North Table Mountain, or Table for short. We roll past the Coors Brewery, taking in the heavy smell of brewing hops. It is mid January and it has snowed on and off for the last month. During the drive to the parking area we speculate whether or not the cliff will be dry, let alone warm enough to climb. As we wind through the neighborhood and onto the dirt road leading to the parking lot, we decide we don't care because we'll be climbing outside for the first time in a month. I take a gamble and leave the down jacket in the car, knowing the short approach won't kill me if I have to do it a second time that day. The trail is surprisingly dry, as is the cliff, which only reveals patches of snow concealed in the darkest north facing gullies. We warm up on *Mr. Squirrel Places a Nut*, an iconic Table route, and while basking in the sun at the base, I forget what time of year it is and strip down to a t-shirt. Looking around, I notice that most of the other climbers at the cliff have done the same.

As the day progresses, I stop trying to worry about what holds might be considered "on" or "off", as many routes are near ledges or gullies, and try to appreciate the sport lines for how the first ascentionist had envisioned the line. Vertical faces with sequential, technical cruxes reveal themselves as we pick our way down the wall. Small, flat edges and bulging arêtes with sloping sidepulls give way to a surprising pump. We pass by a steady row of aesthetic arêtes and jam a few of the more obscure but delightful cracks. Some climbers have been known to call Table a small, dumpy chosspile that has mostly contrived, over-bolted sport routes, but many more will say that there are far more redeeming qualities about the area than bad ones. The Golden Cliffs are one of the most popular sport climbing areas in the Front Range because no where else in the Front Range do so many moderate sport routes below 5.11 exist in such concentration. With such close proximity to Boulder and the Denver metro area, North Table Mountain is one of the premier winter hangs.

Table locals have been waiting a long time for an updated guidebook, one that includes the nearly 100 new routes that have been added over the last decade, increasing the routes by nearly one and a half times. I have had a lot of fun climbing here over the years and have enjoyed meeting new climbers every time I go. I also enjoyed talking to some of the original route developers and filling in some of the historical gaps. I hope this book serves you well and to see you around the cliff this winter.

— Jason Haas

Preface

Being the oldest of the precocious and eclectic group of kids with whom I discovered climbing, I felt an unusual amount of pressure to get my driver's license as soon as possible. I suppose we must have struck other climbers as an odd group: Ben (not me) proudly flaunted his long pony tail and hippy-throwback cords; Chris did his best to scare any small children we encountered with a spiked Mohawk and leather steel-studded wrist and neck bands; Boulos was perhaps the most unpredictable of the group, prone to running around the climbing gym swinging large cams above his head; I rounded out the group with my oddly nerdy yet reckless disposition. It is highly doubtful that the four of us would have said a word to one another were it not for the common obsession with climbing, which united us in an unlikely brotherhood. Before I acquired my license, a few of us would ride our bikes from Boulder to Eldorado Canyon after school, all of us tossing in our meager resources to form a piecemeal rack. At the time, I thought sketching out on lead with no gear was a normal climbing experience. Given this predisposition to poor adolescent decision-making, however, we still quickly exhausted the routes we could climb in Eldorado with a rack of quickdraws and a mismatched handful of nuts and hexes.

It was for this reason that I begged my father, with the apparent weight of the futures of us all on my shoulders, to take me to the DMV on the morning of my sixteenth birthday. I still remember the DMV clerk handing over that long sought after symbol of freedom. No longer were we dependent on our bikes to take us to Eldo after school.

Just a few months earlier, my climbing mentor Todd McMillen introduced Boulos and me to the Golden Cliffs. Astonished by the sane nature of the climbing there, we all soon explored more of it. My parents, thinking I enjoyed some sort of steep hiking, usually handed over the keys to their '88 Toyota Tercel with the misplaced fear that I might recklessly damage their *car*. They had no idea that the use of their car allowed us to actually go to safer places to climb. I remember taking my first lead fall on a bolt at the Golden Cliffs; the feeling of relief was overwhelming—it wasn't the blindly placed nut that held the first lead fall I ever took.

Pleasant weekends in Golden filled that winter and spring. We survived unscathed, thanks in no small part to Todd's patient mentoring, with which I did my best to pass on to my buddies, and the safe and friendly attributes of the crag. Wonderful routes like *Deck Chairs on the Titanic* and *Brown Cloud Arête* stand out amongst my many memories; wonderful gym-like sequences, crisp holds, the occasional jam, clean rock, aesthetic movement and safe leading typify many of Table's numerous great lines.

In hindsight, the only thing the Golden Cliffs were missing back then was a reasonable trail and a decent guidebook. Many thanks go to the Access Fund and their volunteers for replacing the old trail that hugged a barbed wire fence and shot straight uphill. Now, 15 years after my introduction to climbing here, I hope this guidebook will complement not only the Access Fund's efforts, but also the efforts of the numerous individuals who spent countless hours and dollars replacing rusty old bolts and developing many more routes since the last publication of a guidebook for this area.

—— Ben Schneider

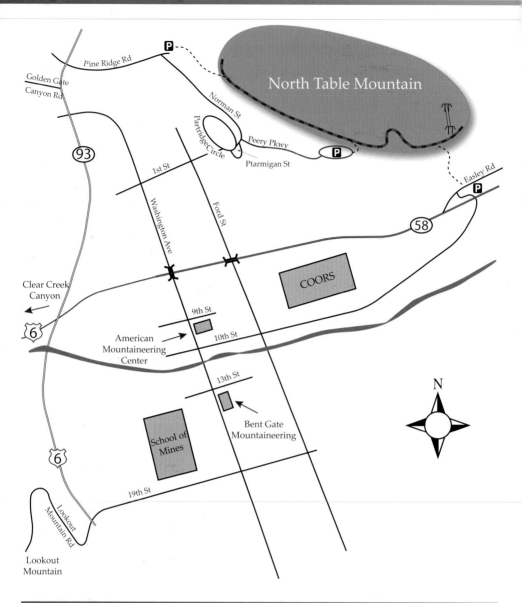

North Table Mountain

Pine Ridge Rd

Golden Gate
Canyon Rd

Norman St

93

Partridge Circle

Peery Pkwy

Ptarmigan St

1st St

Washington Ave

Ford St

Easley Rd

58

Clear Creek
Canyon

6

COORS

9th St

American
Mountaineering
Center

10th St

13th St

Bent Gate
Mountaineering

N

6

School of
Mines

19th St

Lookout
Mountain Rd

Lookout
Mountain

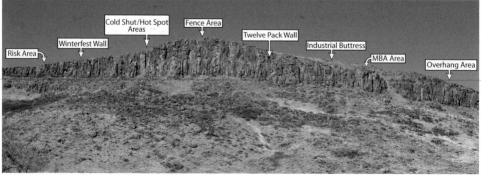

Risk Area · Winterfest Wall · Cold Shut/Hot Spot Areas · Fence Area · Twelve Pack Wall · Industrial Buttress · MBA Area · Overhang Area

From the Denver Area – Take I-70 west to exit #265 and head west on Colorado Highway 58 for 4.5 miles to the Washington Avenue exit, which is just beyond the Coors Brewery. Turn right onto Washington Avenue. After four blocks, turn right onto 1st Street and follow it for three blocks until it terminates at Partridge Circle. Take another right onto Partridge Circle and then take the first left onto Ptarmigan Street. Follow Ptarmigan St. around a sweeping right hand curve as it parallels the cliff to a T-intersection with Peery Parkway. Veer left onto Peery Pky, driving past a "Dead End" sign to where the road ends at the dirt entrance to Golden Cliffs Open Space. Follow the lower, right fork to the main parking area.

From Boulder – Drive south on Colorado Highway 93 (which turns into Foothills Rd in the town of Golden) and turn left onto Washington Avenue before reaching US-6/CO-58 and the heart of Golden. Go three blocks and turn left onto 1st St. Follow this for another three blocks until it terminates at Partridge Circle. Turn right and then take the first left onto Ptarmigan Street. Follow Ptarmigan St around a sweeping right hand curve as it parallels the cliff to a T-intersection with Peery Parkway. Veer left onto Peery Pky, driving past a "Dead End" sign to where the road ends at the dirt entrance to Golden Cliffs Open Space. Follow the lower, right fork to the main parking area.

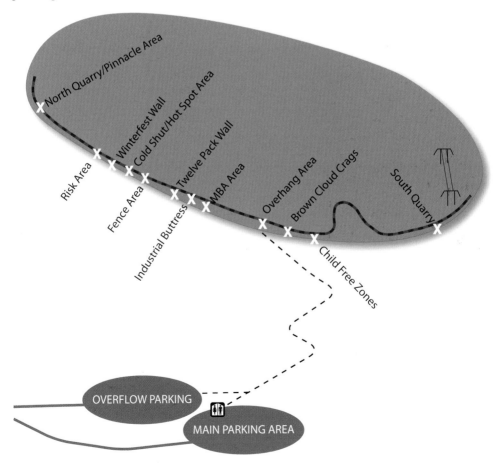

Cliff Layout and Route Colors

Routes are listed linearly from left to right starting at the far end with North Quarry and extending right to South Quarry, with the main wall in between. While the approach trail reaches the main wall at the end of the Overhang Area and route #224, *This Ain't Naturita* Pilgrim (p.85), the book is more user friendly and easier to understand if the routes go left to right the same way a person reads a book left to right. We tried the other way and it was not conducive to quickly figuring out where you are. Anytime an approach trail comes in from the right instead of the left, confusion is bound to arise and so we did the best we could to remedy this, specifically with the addition of the top banner representing the main wall. The moving yellow box in the banner indicates where specific routes are located to help pinpoint your location along the main wall.

To also help identify the type of route climbers are looking for, description photos have yellow lines drawn in to indicate sport and toprope routes, blue lines identify trad routes, and green lines are for the few boulder problems that exist. Mixed lines that are partially bolted are also blue because they still require trad gear. The route number color in the text description also corresponds with which type of route it is for quick identification.

Route Grades and Quality

The authors personally climbed 100% of the routes at North Table Mountain in an attempt to help normalize grade and quality ratings. In addition, consensus opinions were taken from countless other climbers who have done specific routes in order to create an average of opinions in terms of both difficulty and quality. Everyone's climbing experience, height, personal strengths/weaknesses and preferences vary so please take these ratings with a grain of salt. They are merely an attempt to help guide climbers towards specific routes that they may find most enjoyable at a specific grade level and are only in comparison to other Table Mountain routes and not measured against nearby legendary climbing areas like Eldorado Canyon and the Flatirons, or with other great nearby sport climbing crags like Clear Creek Canyon or Boulder Canyon.

No stars depicts a route with few redeeming qualities, whether it is a grungy gully/dihedral system, very chossy, or a horribly contrived squeeze job. While this is completely subjective, most climbers will prefer to walk on by.

★ Indicates a route of average quality that offers enjoyable, but forgettable climbing. These routes are generally worthwhile, but nothing about them stands out as being unique or memorable. You don't regret doing it, but generally consider these pitches to be nothing more than mileage.

★★ A good route that has provocative movement on quality rock.

★★★ This is a great route that should not be missed and is a local favorite. The route has mental and physical challenges that leave one craving more. If you only have a short amount of time to spend here, these are the not to be missed routes that truly illustrate everything North Table Mountain has to offer.

Equipment

Most routes range from 50-70ft in height, although some shorter as well as taller routes do exist. As a general rule, 10 quickdraws and a 50meter rope will get you up and off of most of the routes here. When a taller route requires a longer rope or extra draws, it is duly noted in the route description. Quite often, trad routes can easily be toproped from the anchors of nearby sport routes, but for those wishing to lead them, a standard trad rack (SR) includes: a set of nuts, a single set of cams to three inches, and a few double length runners or quickdraws. Trad routes are marked with a blue line in the description photos to help distinguish them from the yellow sport routes. Trad routes requiring additional gear outside of the standard rack mentioned above will be noted under the specific route description.

An accurate bolt count is listed below each specific route, but a bolt may have been missed, or unfortunately, retrobolts may have been added. Try to confirm the number of bolts on a specific route before climbing with exactly the correct number of quickdraws, but regardless of the off chance of an additional retrobolt, it may be wise to bring an extra draw anyway in the event one is dropped. Also, bolt counts do not include the anchor so be sure to bring a little something extra for that.

Weather – When to Climb

The weather at North Table Mountain has created such a user-friendly place to climb that it is one of the most popular crags on the Front Range, particularly during the winter months. The southern exposure along the majority of the cliff gets more sun, even through the shortest winter days, than any other local area, allowing climbers to bask in the warmth, oftentimes climbing in t-shirts. Snow quickly melts off the faces and approach trail, rarely stopping climbers from enjoying an afternoon of cranking, even on chilly winter days. Spring and autumn are also considered prime climbing time, as the days are longer and weather more stable. Because of the amount of sun the cliff gets, summer can be scorching hot, however climbs around the Risk Area, Winterfest Wall, and Fence Area stay shaded until noon and can offer a nice morning climbing spot.

Fixed Gear

Many of the original sport routes were comprised of coldshut anchors, some welded shut and some unwelded. Old gear should always be approached with great caution, especially unwelded cold shuts (like on *Electrocuticles*), which can open under even moderate forces generated by short falls. You alone are responsible for your safety, so use your best judgment when trusting old gear. Climbers that are both skilled and knowledgeable in how to replace unsafe hardware are encouraged to do so using stainless steel bolts and hangers only. Please also camouflage the hangers with a paint color that blends in with the rock. For those without that knowledge or skill, please know that it is a thankless job that climbers do using their own money and equipment out of the kindness of their hearts. If you see someone replacing old bolts or know someone who has done it, please express your appreciation for all their hard work.

Top Anchor Wear – who will replace them?

When I climb at North Table Mountain, my quickdraws or trad rack is always accompanied by a wrench. I tighten the occasional spinner, but more often than not I deal with top anchors that show dangerous signs of wear. Deep grooves can be worn into the steel because of friction caused by countless ropes being dragged back and forth over the metal when climbers toprope or are lowered through the anchor. Because the area is so beginner friendly, this problem has become more of a major concern here than virtually anywhere else on the Front Range. Please rappel off of the anchors when you are done climbing the route. Weighting both ends of the rope with a static pull does not cause unnecessary wear on the anchor. If you are unsure how to do this ask another climber nearby, or if you see a beginner lowering through the anchor, please take the time to educate him or her. The far greater concern however is toproping through the anchor because it causes more friction for a longer amount of time, rubbing grooves into the anchor and weakening the overall strength of it, which will eventually cause the anchor to fail. If toproping a route, do so through quickdraws attached to the anchor and never through the anchor itself. A grave reality is that those who prefer to lower through the anchor are generally not the ones replacing worn out anchors. Please ensure that replacement efforts do not dwindle as those replacing the anchors feel their efforts are unappreciated, especially when they see their newly replaced anchor needing replacing in as little as two seasons. Please take this into consideration if you prefer to lower through the anchors, especially if you are not involved in any replacement initiatives. If you do know of an anchor that needs attention, please contact the authors through their website www.fixedpin.com or an organization such as the American Safe Climbing Association or Anchor Replacement Initiative who can get in contact with local volunteers who can replace the anchor. Ken Trout has generously taken the initiative to replace numerous anchors on the more popular routes with lowering stations from Home Depot. Time will tell if these are better than traditional setups, or if they simply fall prey to grooves like all the other anchors.

Loose Rock

North Table Mountain does not deserve the chossy reputation it once had; the majority of the rock itself on the cliff is quite bomber and breaking holds is rare on the more traveled lines. The real danger comes from loose blocks in rarely traveled dihedral systems and on ledges, as well as along the rim on top of the cliff. The majority of loose rock has been removed from the more popular lines, including a 500lb death flake that fell from *Monkey Puzzle* with only a few gentle taps of a hammer! The flake pierced the ground, standing on end rather than smashing into a million tiny pieces. Be particularly careful about loose blocks if topping out and walking off a route or if establishing a toprope, as even the smallest-sized rock can have grave consequences for other hikers and climbers moving about the base of the cliff. If you establish a new route, please be sure to remove as much loose rock as possible before making it available to the rest of the climbing community.

Ethics – Is that a soapbox he's on?

In Colorado's Front Range, North Table Mountain is often the first outside climbing area new climbers experience once they venture out from the indoor climbing gyms. That is exactly why this area should be considered a cornerstone in climbing ethics, a prime example of a cliff, owned by the Access Fund, which is user friendly to beginners and the first exposure to positive ethics they will experience. It is unfortunate however, that Table does not live up to such a lofty goal. Retrobolting, where bolts have been added to preexisting climbs, bolting cracks which take natural protection, and squeezing in lines that encroach on other routes have run rampant at the cliff, setting a bad example for newcomers to our sport, who will eventually branch out to other climbing areas and take their climbing ethics with them. It is not so much that the majority of climbers at Table Mountain believe in these things, but if new climbers are taught that they are acceptable, or that they are the norm, then they may try to apply them elsewhere. Through education, that is the sort of thing we as a community need to try and prevent.

While it is fun to climb new routes, no one needs to climb every route. If the route is over your head, please do not bring it down to your level by retrobolting it. Why not toprope the route instead? Does every route have to be lead? Admire those that came before you, using much more rudimentary gear than what is available today, and accomplishing climbs that may be deemed unsafe by some. It is an expression of their style to choose to place or not to place bolts, just like it would be an expression of your style to establish a new route with or without bolts.

Bolting cracks can also be considered dumbing a route down to the most accessible level. It is true that not everyone has trad gear, but it is also true most trad routes here can easily be toproped from the anchors on a nearby climb. Bolts scar the rock, and bolted cracks spark bolt wars, which only lead to more destruction and scarring of the rock.

New Routes

As mentioned above, adding squeeze job routes is unacceptable. Consider if the proposed line will be a positive addition to the already bountiful amount of sport routes at Table. Routes that use holds on other existing routes are better left as toprope variations. Be sure to remove all the loose rock from the new route and only use stainless steel bolts and hangers (no coldshuts) so that they last longer. Hangers should also be painted a camouflaged color to blend in with the rock prior to installation; the less visual impact fixed gear has, the better.

Request for Comments and New Route Information

Any guidebook is a work in progress, building on the books and information that came before it. This book is no exception. Correct first ascent information was tracked down using a multitude of sources, but errors may still exist. If you know of any historical details, have new route information, or would like to submit general comments, please send them to us via our website www.fixedpin.com.

Amenities

Camping

There is no camping at North Table Mountain and unfortunately there are not any legal and free camping spots along Colorado's Front Range. The closest camping option is the Golden Clear Creek RV Park located at 1400 10th St, which has a few camping sites available for $20 per night. Another option is Golden Gate State Park, http://parks.state.co.us/Parks/goldengatecanyon, which is 14 miles northwest of Golden. Take Highway 93 north from Golden for 1.0mi to Golden Gate Canyon Road. Turn left and follow it for 13mi to the park entrance, which has tent sites for $14 a night with toilets, showers, and some electrical hookup sites. The state park also has shelters and backcountry camping for up to six people for $8 per night. Numerous nice hotels and bed and breakfasts exist in Golden. Cheap hotels are abundant in the area as well, especially the closer one goes to Denver.

Groceries and Restaurants

There are several grocery stores in Golden, including a King Soopers, Safeway, and a Golden Natural Foods for those who are health conscious. Golden's quaint downtown also contains numerous fine-dining experiences, ranging from excellent Asian cuisine to wood fired pizza at Woody's.

Gear Shops and Climbing Gyms

The main climbing shop in town is Bent Gate Mountaineering, which is located on Washington Ave near the corner of 13th St. Note that Bent Gate is CLOSED on Saturdays in honor of the Sabbath. There is also Neptune Mountaineering and Boulder Mountaineering in Boulder, Wilderness Exchange in Denver, as well as an REI in both Boulder and Denver.

There may not be any other place in the country with such a high density of climbing gyms as the Boulder/Denver Area for those pesky rainy days. Rock'n & Jam'n, Paradise, and Thrillseekers are all located in Denver and are the closest gyms to Golden. Boulder also has the Boulder Rock Club, Spot Bouldering Gym, and C.A.T.S. for some good indoor plastic pulling.

Entertainment and Diversions

Golden is not without its quaint mountain town feel and a plethora of fun diversions to choose from on rest days. The American Mountaineering Center on the corner of 10th St and Washington Ave, which houses the American Alpine Club (and library), Colorado Mountain Club, and American Mountain Guides Association, should not be missed. The building has beautiful climbing photographs lining the walls, only surpassed in historical nostalgia by the Bradford Washburn museum. That's not even mentioning all the exciting climbers to talk to about various expeditions from around the world, or lounging about watching free climbing movies in the AAC library. If you want to stay active, but the tips need to heal, there is a great whitewater play park in town, but if you want to soak up the full value of a rest day and avoid the climbing scene, the Coors Brewery is worth visiting. Don't miss the free samples at the end of the tour! Golden also has several museums and western historical sites in and around the town.

The American Mountaineering Center

Trash

A recent BLM study showed that climbers were one of the lowest impact recreational groups in terms of trash. Please help continue this trend by packing out everything, including used athletic tape, sports bar wrappers and cigarette butts, even if it's not yours.

Dogs

According to the BLM, dogs are the largest complaint made about climbers, and dogs are more present than ever at the crags today. If you bring your dog to the cliff, please keep in mind that there is a subdivision in close proximity. If your dog does not respond to voice commands or requires constant supervision, which you cannot give while climbing/belaying, please keep it on a leash. This will ensure that it does not chase wildlife or other dogs and does not roam the cliff base where it will undoubtedly bother other climbers by straying onto their ropes or begging for food. Additionally, whether your dog is leashed or not, please pick up its poop and pack it out, just as you have to at any other Open Space. Dogs demonstrating threatening behavior such as growling, harassing, or acting territorial towards other dogs or people is unacceptable and is an issue that needs to be addressed by the dog owner immediately rather than waiting for the other person to get upset. Finally, please do not leave your dog tied up at the base of a route while you head off to climb somewhere else out of sight.

Private Land – climbing in an urban setting

While the Access Fund owns the majority of the climbing area, the cliff stands like an armory wall above a large suburban community below. Traditionally the residents of the neighborhood, particularly those with property just below the cliffs, have had a tense relationship with climbers. Relations have gotten better over the years, but please follow a few simple guidelines going to and from the crag including obeying the residential speed limit. Understandably, the increased traffic is a large concern for those residents with small children. The parking area is managed by the Golden Police Department, who are kind enough to open the gates at dawn and lock them up at dusk. Be sure to be out of the parking area before the night patrol or you may be locked in for the night. Also, please only park at the main parking area or the overflow area if the main lot is full. Do not park on the neighborhood streets and please act responsibly and respectfully around the neighborhood residents.

Natural History
Natural Hazards
During warm sunny days, particularly in summer and fall, rattlesnakes can be found sunning themselves on the rocks along the base of the cliff. They also like to hide in bushes or under shaded boulders while cooling themselves. Keep an eye out and be sure to leave them alone and walk away if one is seen. Mountain lions have also periodically appeared along the mesa, although these elusive cats are not often spotted. The main times of day to be on alert are at dawn and dusk.

Other Flora/Fauna Interests
Much of the mesa surrounding North Table Mountain is covered in shrubs such as wild snowberry, mountain mahogany, wild plum, and skunkbush sumac. The surrounding area is also home to other bushes including cactus, yucca, skunkweed, wild alyssum grass, currant and chokecherry.

Over 50 species of birds have been spotted in the area, including raptors, which occasionally nest on the cliffs, particularly near *Winter Warmer*. When this happens, there are occasional seasonal closures for the raptors, although there are none in effect currently. Please be sure to keep an eye out for signs indicating a closure and respect the closure if one is in place.

Geology
Somewhere between 35-65 million years ago a ten-mile long lake of liquid lava flowed down from Ralston Dike, three miles north of Golden, and extended all the way south to Green Mountain. Later, two additional capping lava flows composed of what is officially known as Table Mountain Shoshonite, a potassium-rich basalt, oozed over the original lava flow leaving behind Table Mountain in its wake. Eventually, Clear Creek carved a large channel through the main formation, splitting it into South and North Table Mountain, with nearly a 1,000-acre mesa atop North Table.

This aphanitic-porphyritic hornblende basalt is much harder than that of other climbing areas like Smith Rock or more locally known Penitente Canyon, but it does not have pockets like at those areas. While portions of the cliff can reach as high as 150ft at the southern end and 100ft along the west face, most of the climbs are much shorter, comprised of vertical, thin-face cruxes on very compact rock. The reason for this is that the lava flows consist of a coarsely grained, crystalline rock in the lower and middle sections, while the upper section has finer-grained (poorly consolidated) crystals, resulting in a broken, crumbly upper edge to the crag, which is most apparent on the taller portions of the cliff. Because of the multiple capping flows of lava, there are actually two separate lava bands, which are easily distinguished on the southern end of the cliff where the approach trail reaches the wall. The lower band has a few climbs along the Lower Child Free Zone, but the majority of the climbing exists on the upper level, which spans nearly two miles.

Welcome to Walk - Climbing History by Richard Berk

Historically, The Golden Cliffs at North Table Mountain were used for hunting by the local Indian tribes and for grazing and mining by the subsequent settlers. South Table Mountain has seen similar historic uses but has the added color of being the site of a cafe/dance hall and funicular railway in the early 1900's. After being abandoned by it's last owner, the Klu Klux Klan used it until an arsonist burned it to the ground.

In late 1986, my brother and I began to consider the rock climbing potential offered by the Table Mountains. We began with Castle Rock on South Table Mountain; our first and only route there ascended a light colored section of the cliff overlooking Golden. Though the exposure looking down over Golden was great, the rock was loose and the climbing mediocre at best.

Not completely put off by our foray up Castle Rock, Scott one day wandered up the old fence line on North Table Mountain, ending up somewhere right of middle of what is now the Winter Warmer area. He slipped on his shoes, picked a route that looked fairly straightforward and headed up. Named *Abortion Central* (5.7 X), the rock was as worthless as our route up South Table. However, while descending, he noticed that much of the cliff looked far better. He and I returned a few days later and put up *Raw Fish and Rice*; it was at this point that we realized the potential for short but quality climbs.

Richard Berk hand drilling one of the original routes

We asked around trying to find any information on previous climbers as we knew that there were cavers that had used North Table Mountain for rappelling practice, and we found a few pitons hammered into cracks near the top of the cliff to the north of the Winter Warmer area. We knew people had been climbing in Clear Creek since probably the 1950's so it was hard to imagine no one had been on North Table Mountain. But, for the next four years it was ours.

In the fall and winter of 1987, the pace of route development picked up. School friends Jeffery Brown, Dave Hart and occasionally a few others joined us. We had a clear view of the crags from the Colorado School of Mines, where we all did our best to attend classes, and often all it took was a wishful glance between classes and in ten minutes we would be heading up the fence line trail. On a good day in the winter you could ski laps on the back of Lookout Mountain (Mt. Zion) in the morning and climb on Table in a t-shirt in the afternoon.

17

We began with obvious crack routes: *Heidi Hi, Shadow of a Hangdog, Fast Boat to China, Bush Loves Detroit* and *Killian's Dead*. It was obvious, however, that much of the Golden Cliffs' potential lay in the faces. We were soon pounding out 3/8-inch holes and filling them with what we hoped was quality hardware. The early bolted lines were routes like *Politicians, Priests and Body Bags, Salad Bar*, and *Flight 67 to Stockholm*.

By 1989 we were trying hard to get others up to the rock, and a few other groups made it out now and then. We bouldered frequently at Morrison and mentioned it to several of the regulars, one of whom was Ken Trout. After several attempts, Scott convinced Ken to go take a look. Some time later I headed up to find three power drills going at the same time; things were changing.

Ken Trout published a Rock & Ice mini guide (1992). Along with the late Alan Nelson, Guy Lord, Tod Anderson, Richard Wright, Mark Rolofson and others, the Golden Cliffs were transformed from a nice locals spot to a great, easily accessible, highly used sport-climbing venue.

As the area's popularity grew the inevitable conflicts between neighbors, landowners, and climber began to flare up. It began with neighborhood parking issues and grew to at least one closure of the area. Golden City Council meetings pitted neighbors against climbers and the Access Fund eventually stepped into the fray.

Scott Berk on Salad Bar

No history of the Golden Cliffs would be complete without mentioning one more person. It is likely no one would be climbing there now if it were not for him. A friend and I were lounging in my van after climbing one day. An older man approached us down the side of North Table Mountain. He was dressed in slacks and a white t-shirt, with blood dripping down one arm and was carrying a plastic grocery bag in the other. He walked up to the van and asked us if we needed any help. I was unsure how to answer him, but when he introduced himself as Mr. Peery, I realized whom we were talking to. At the time he still owned most of the land we had been climbing on. The bag was full of wild asparagus - amazing stuff. At one point he said he had lived in Golden for nearly 70 years. I observed that he must have seen many changes in that time. He confirmed that he had in fact instigated many of those changes. He was one of those people whose word you just take without question.

At the time, there had been some conflict between the neighborhood and climbers about parking. As we said goodbye to Mr. Peery he noted that if anyone gave us problems about parking to tell him or her that Mr. Peery said we could park where we wanted.

Sometime around 1997, Mr. Peery donated the climbing crags, the parking areas, and the region of the approach trail to the Access Fund. As Richard Wright wrote, "pretty amazing. Particularly so when you figure how many people in the greater Denver metropolitan area use North Table Mountain for a quick after work pitch or just to pull down a dozen routes in a day. I cannot think of another example where a single individual's generosity has so directly affected so many climbers - in a good way!" Mr. Peery passed away several years ago.

Scott Berk on Flight 67 to Stockholm

When we began exploring North Table Mountain there was a simple sign posted at the old fence-line trail head that read "Welcome to Walk." That sign was Mr. Peery's.

TOP TWENTY TABLE SPORT ROUTES

1 Kevin Spies the Line 5.6 ■	11 Bullet the Brown Cloud 5.11b ■
2 Honey I Shrunk the Hemmorrhoids 5.7 ■	12 Crawling Up Roseanne's Belly 5.11b ■
3 Brain Cloud 5.9 ■	13 Rebel Yell 5.11b ■
4 Deck Chairs on the Titanic 5.9 ■	14 Industrial Disease 5.11c ■
5 Brown Cloud Arete 5.10a ■	15 Interstellar Overdrive 5.11c ■
6 F.A.T.A.L. 5.10b ■	16 Mr. Squirrel Places a Nut 5.11c ■
7 Crack and Face Route 5.10c ■	17 Mrs. Hen Places a Peck 5.11d ■
8 Sunset Arete 5.10d ■	18 Monkey Puzzle 5.12a ■
9 Winter Warmer 5.10d ■	19 The Mohare Edge 5.12b ■
10 Major Bolt Achievement 5.11a ■	20 Pseudo Bullet 5.12b ■

North Quarry
← 1 mi

#85   #100   ⤸ Access Fund
Property Line

Broad
Gully

#150

NORTH QUARRY/PINNACLE AREA

Approach: To reach the parking lot, turn east onto Pine Ridge Rd. from CO-93. Go one block and turn left at the stop sign. Follow Wyoming St. another block to the trailhead on the left. From here, hike up the trail behind the houses, which runs into a dirt road. Leave the road by turning right onto a trail just before the water tank. Hike 300yrds to a point directly below the cliff and head up a scree field to the right of the large, detached, chossy pinnacle that sits just in front of the cliff line. For toprope access, head up a gully 150ft left of all the routes.

1 Unknown A 5.10c ★★

This is the far left bolted slab with old school bed frame style hangers, just as the cliff becomes tall enough to be worth climbing.

Gear: 4 bolts   2-bolt anchor

❷ Wide Pride 5.9 ★★

A pure offwidth, too bad it isn't longer. Pull an overhanging start via several wedged blocks and grunt up the offwidth. Break left near the top to an anchor in the middle of the face.

Gear: SR to #5 Camalot   2-bolt anchor

3 Unknown B 5.12a ★★

Begin on a boulder five feet right of *Wide Pride* and attempt to stick clip the ridiculously high first bolt. Work up the delicate slab and bust out the left side of the roof. Continue up the left-arcing bolt line along a layback crack. Another bolt should be added below the first one so as to protect the crux start that currently has bone breaking potential for people unable to reach the first bolt even with a stick clip.

Gear: 4 bolts   2-bolt anchor

#224
#212
Gully
#264
South Quarry
1mi

4 Catching the Quarry 5.11a ★★ ❑
Climb a slab to pass the large roof on the right. Crimp past the remaining coldshut bolts to the anchor.
Gear: 5 bolts   2-bolt anchor
FA: Tod Anderson

5 Burly Man 5.11a ★★★ ❑
Gymnastically finesse your way up a gaping right-facing dihedral and scramble up some jumbled blocks to a huge roof. Traverse out the wide, left side. Pull into the offwidth at the lip and scuttle up to the summit. Use the anchors on the following route.
Gear: SR to #5 Camalot   nearby anchor

6 Unknown C 5.11d ★★★ ❑
Begin immediately right of *Burly Man*. Climb a hand crack up to the right side of the roof. Pull hard into the hanging dihedral and work out the technical stem moves below the anchor.
Gear: 2 bolts, SR to #4 Camalot   2-bolt anchor

7 Boobalaty 5.8 ★ ❑
Chimney up the dark slot five feet right of *Unknown C*. Use the anchors on *Cracking Up*.
Gear: SR to #5 Camalot   nearby anchor

8 Unknown D 5.8 ★ ❑
Climb the first 20ft of either *Boobalaty* or *Cracking Up* and then follow a thin crack between those two routes, which widens into an offwidth flake near the top. Use the anchor on *Cracking Up*.
Gear: SR to #5 Camalot   shared anchor

9 Cracking Up 5.11b ★ ❑
Work up a broken crack system that arcs left into a horizontal at mid-height. Crimp up the bolt protected face above to the anchor.
Gear: 2 bolts, SR   2-bolt anchor
FA: Tod Anderson

Broad
Gully

North Quarry
← 1 mi

#85   #100   ↰ Access Fund
Property Line

#150

#224
#212
Gully
#264
South Quarry
1mi →

10 Rancid 5.10b ★

Move 60ft right of *Cracking Up*, around a chossy buttress and scree-filled gully. Clip up the old school bolts to a fist crack finish.

Gear: 5 bolts   2-bolt anchor
FA: Deaun Schovajsa, Dave Gottenborg 1994

Jason Haas, *Burly Man* (5.11a), p.21   photo: Ben Schneider

23

North Quarry
← 1 mi

#85 #100 ↰ Access Fund
Property Line

Broad
Gully →

#150

RISK AREA

Approach: This is the leftmost section of the cliff at the main area and can be identified from far away by a second cliff band forming below the climbing routes. The wall is quite short here and routes can easily be toproped by scrambling up to the left. The trail breaks down at this point and people must either scramble up onto the mesa or down below the second cliff band in order to keep hiking left.

11 Purposefully Put In 5.7
Start 20ft left of *Little Green Apples*. Work up a short left-facing corner, traversing up and left along a crack. Finish in the low-angled dihedral.
Gear: SR to #4 Camalot   Walk off

12 Almost Left Out 5.6
(Scraping the Barrel)
Begin five feet right of *Purposefully* and 15ft left of *Little Green Apples*. Follow a finger crack over lichen-covered ledges.
Gear: SR   Walk off

13 Little Green Apples 5.8 ★
This is the furthest left sport route at the Risk Area and the main cliff. Climb the left side of a small, bulging pillar to the anchors on the following route.
Gear: 3 bolts   shared anchor
FA: Alan Nelson 2001

14 My Big Red Catcher's Mitt 5.10a ★
Climb the right side of the pillar past a long layback flake. The route is 5.10d if the obvious stem out right is avoided at the start.
Gear: 3 bolts   2-bolt anchor
FA: Guy Lords

Geoff Elson, *Wide Pride* (5.9), p. 20

photo: Ben Schneider

North Quarry
← 1 mi

#85 #100

Broad
Gully

Access Fund
Property Line

#150

15 Uncle Shorty 5.8- ★★

Move 10ft right of the previous route to the next pillar. Jam the off-fingers/tight-hands crack on the left side of the pillar, clipping bolts for the variation below.
Gear: SR or 3 bolts   2-bolt anchor
Variation: Mama Midget 5.10b
A bolted contrivance. Climb part of the crack and part of the face over a bulge at mid-height. *FA: Alan Nelson.*

16 Daddy Dwarf 5.10d ★★★

Oppositional sidepulls up an A-framed face leads to a slanting shelf at mid-height. Blast up the reachy crux via the crack on the right just before the top.
Gear: 3 bolts   2-bolt anchor   FA: Alan Nelson

17 Stupid Human Trick V0

Climb rounded slopers on a slender pinnacle 10ft right of *Daddy Dwarf*. Bail out halfway up at a ledge or continue up to the top (5.8).

18 Unknown E 5.8 ★

Climb the crack just left of *The Perfect Ten*. Move around a bulge near the top, place a directional, and use the anchor above *Perfect Ten*.
Gear: SR   nearby anchor

19 The Perfect Ten 5.10a ★★★

Crisp edges and fissures appear exactly where needed on this otherwise smooth, burnt red face. For full value, avoid the crack on the previous route as much as possible.
Gear: 4 bolts   2-bolt anchor

20 Not 5.10b ★★★

A great counterpart to *Perfect Ten* with a slightly harder start. Flow up the face to a ledge and then take the finger crack in the open book to the top.
Gear: 4 bolts   shared anchor

21 Risk of Injection 5.11c ★★

This extended boulder problem is on from the word go. Slap up the short, burly, overhanging prow just right of *Not*.
Gear: 2 bolts   chain anchors
FA: Guy Lords

22 Serendipity 5.9- ★

Finesse your way up an open book just right of *Risk of Injection*. Stem over a small bulge and continue up ledges to the top. Despite the lichen, it's not a bad climb.
Gear: SR   Walk off

23 This Bolt's For You 5.11a ★★

Balance up the delicate arête, fighting the barn door along the way.
Gear: 4 bolts   2-bolt anchor
FA: Tod Anderson, Richard Wright 1995

Laramie Duncan, *The Perfect Ten* (5.10a), opposite page   photo: Ben Schneider

North Quarry
← 1 mi

#85   #100   ← Access Fund
Property Line

Broad
Gully

#150

24 Chillin' and Drillin' 5.11d ★★★ ❑

Sustained stemming and technical footwork in a right-facing dihedral leads to a roof. Traverse left underneath it to merge with the previous route at the last bolt.
Gear: 4 bolts   shared anchor
FA: Mike Morely, Alan Nelson 2004

25 This Bone's For You 5.9 ★★ ❑

Begin between *Chillin' and Drillin'* and *Chimney Route*. Prance up the juggy face to the top. Use long slings on the anchor.
Gear: 6 bolts   2-bolt anchor
FA: Alan Nelson 2001

26 Chimney Route 5.8 ★ ❑

Chimney up the first half before switching into a jam/layback for the upper fist crack. Use anchors on the preceding route.
Gear: SR to #4 Camalot

27 Mettle Detector 5.10d ★★ ❑

This is the short, right-facing dihedral squeezed between *Chimney Route* and *Hand Crack*. Stem up the corner, protecting with thin gear until it is possible to move left on top of a hanging pillar. Follow the crack to a bolted anchor. Will get better with traffic.
Gear: SR   2-bolt anchor
FA: Alan Nelson

28 Hand Crack 5.8 ★★★ ❑

For such a perfect jamming crack, one would expect a more creative name. Float up perfect hands in a changing corner to the anchor on *Mettle Detector*.
Gear: SR   shared anchor

29 Unknown F 5.7 ❑

Climb a fist crack 15ft right of *Hand Crack*, which widens into an offwidth. Stem the corner to the top, descending from anchors above *Mettle Detector*.
Gear: SR to #5 Camalot   nearby anchor

#224
#212
Gully
#264
South Quarry
1mi

30 Al and Mike's Frosty Little Adventure 5.8 ★

Move 10ft right of the previous route to a low undercut. Surmount the undercut and follow a crack that jogs up and right through a right-angling groove, then peters out at a small roof. Traverse right to bypass the overhang, and then up and back left to the top, belaying on gear. (no photo)

Gear: SR   nearby anchor
FA: Alan Nelson, Mike Morley 2004

31 Baby Beeper 5.10b ★★

Scoot 60ft right of *This Bone's For You* to the next bolted line. Climb the left side of an arête with an offset flake/nook.

Gear: 5 bolts   2-bolt anchor

32 Sinister Minister of Evil 5.11c TR ★

Follow a plumb line through the tiered, blocky roofs to *Rope Trick*'s anchor. Three chopped bolts show the way.

FA: Guy Lords

33 Rope Trick 5.10d ★★

A little more deceptive than it looks. Start right of the *Sinister Minister* roofs, traversing left over the top of them to gain the anchor.

Gear: 4 bolts   2-bolt anchor
FA: Guy Lords

34 The Delegate 5.10c ★★

Start just right of *Rope Trick*. Balancy, tricky sequences with good rests lead to a ledge below a left-facing corner. Stem past a few more bolts to the top.

Gear: 7 bolts   2-bolt anchor
FA: Mark Rolofson 2008

WINTERFEST WALL

Approach: Walk 40ft right of *Rope Trick*, around a small buttress to the next clean face with bolts on it. For toprope access, scramble up onto the mesa a little ways left of the Risk Area where the cliff breaks down.

35 Runt 5.8

Work up the broken crack and corner system just left of *Pumcat*. When gear isn't present, reach right to the bolts on *Pumcat*. Beware of loose, crumbly rock.
Gear: SR   shared anchor

36 Pumcat 5.10d ★

Begin just right of the grubby *Runt* corner and climb up the face, generously using the dihedral when needed. The first ascentionist intended for the line to force the face; see the variation below.
Gear: 8 bolts   2-bolt anchor
FA: Alan Nelson 2001
Variation: 5.12b ★ Entirely avoid using the dihedral to the left.

37 Twinkletoes 5.11a

This sport route is squeezed between *Pumcat* and *Dweeb*. Bolts are positioned away from the natural line.
Gear: 8 bolts   2-bolt anchor
FA: Alan Nelson 2001

38 Dweeb 5.9+ ★★

Begin in the groove as for *Twinkletoes*, but follow the arcing crack up and right to get into a v-slot, which ends just before the top. This trad line was retrobolted in 2001.
Gear: 7 bolts   shared anchor
Variation: Cat's Meow 5.9+ ★★ Start a few feet right of *Dweeb* and blast straight up through the bolts, joining back with *Dweeb* at the second retrobolt.

39 Photo Art 5.11a ★★ (Jeff's Third Climb)

Start a little right of *Dweeb* and climb a thin tips seam into a right-facing corner. Pull out a small overhang and motor to the top. This route was retrobolted in 2001 by Alan Nelson.
Gear: 8 retrobolts   2-bolt anchor
FA: Jeff Brown 1988

40 Sunset Arête 5.10d ★★★

Climb up a mellow start to gain the right side of the sharp arête, eventually maneuvering onto the left side.
Gear: 8 bolts   2-bolt anchor
FA: Ken and Marsha Trout 1993

41 Unknown G 5.8 ★

Start as for the following route, but when that route takes the fist crack up the pinnacle, move left and scramble up to a hand crack high on the wall. Top out and belay, rappelling off the anchors on *Sunset Arête*.
Gear: SR   nearby anchor

42 Too Dumb to Sleep In 5.8 ★★★

This wide and sinuous crack is found just a few feet left of *Rebel Yell*. Layback or fist jam to the *Rebel Yell* anchor.
Gear: SR to #5 Camalot   shared anchor

#224
#212
Gully
#264
South Quarry
1mi

43 Rebel Yell 5.11b ★★★

Climb excellent features linked by great moves on the promenant arête to the right of *Sunset Arete*. At the last bolt, stick to the slightly contrived line on the arête or move right to easier ground on the other side of the arête, being careful of the rope.

Gear: 5 bolts   2-bolt anchor
FA: T. Anderson, R. Wright, Eric Leonard 1994

44 Driving Over Stella 5.11a ★★

Begin just around the corner from *Rebel Yell*. Moderate jugs and edges lead to a short crux over a slight bulge, followed by more jugs leading to an anchor below a brown and green lichen-covered prow.

Gear: 5 bolts   2-bolt anchor
FA: Ken Trout, Guy Lords 1990

45 Brokendown Shanty 5.8 ★★★

This delicious bombay chimney protects with gear in the back or three retrobolts on the outside. Begin deep inside the chimney and work up positive jams, shuffling out to the second bolt. Good features lead to the anchor.

SR to #4 Camalot or 3 retrobolts   2-bolt anchor

46 The Underachiever 5.11d ★★

This route was horribly sandbagged as 5.9+ in the last guide. Work up a shallow open book immediately left of *Interstellar Overdrive* to a bulging prow. Layback up the prow, pasting your feet to the glassy left wall. Cross over *Interstellar* on the sloping ledge, continuing up the dihedral to anchors on *Psuedo Bullet*. Protection is sparse and scary; it may be best done on TR.

Gear: SR, some bolts on Interstellar may be reached   shared anchor

47 Interstellar Overdrive 5.11c ★★★ ❑

This stellar route with a high first bolt in
a v-slot dihedral can be found 12ft right
of the unmistakable *Brokendown Shanty*
bombay chimney. Gain the first bolt
and climb the clean dihedral employing
a variety of techniques, all the while
remembering this route was first done
on gear. Follow the bolts to the left onto
a clean face atop the dihedral. Bolts were
added by K. Trout and G. Lords in 1991.
Gear: 7 bolts   2-bolt anchor
FA: Dan Schneider 1988

48 Pseudo Bullet 5.12b ★★★ ❑

Pinch and crimp the left side of a fin
sticking out alongside the first three
bolts to gain a much desired ledge.
Catch a rest before battling a second
crux through tiny crimpers and left-
hand arête slaps to the anchor.
Gear: 8 bolts   2-bolt anchor
FA: Dave Twinam, Annette Bunge 1993

49 Bush Loves Detroit 5.8 ★★★   ❑

Anybody with the good sense to climb
cracks will indeed love this route as
much as the Bushes loved the Motor
City. Begin just left of *Roseanne's Belly*
and get onto a ledge below a splitter
dihedral. Jam it all the way to the top,
using the anchor on the following route.
Gear: SR   shared anchor
FA: Scott and Richard Berk 1987
Variation: Start to the right of the
original start and rejoin the regular line
after 15ft or so.

50 Crawling Up Roseanne's Belly ❑
5.11b ★★★

Locate a narrow pillar a few feet right
of *Psuedo Bullet*. Amble up a few bolts
to find out why the bearhugging slaps
up this rounded prow poke fun of this
former comic. Stay with the arête proper
over a small overhang at the top and be
awarded with an anchor just below a
ledge up top.
Gear: 7 bolts   2-bolt anchor
FA: K. and M. Trout, R. Leitner, J. Garber 1991

51 Bimbo in Limbo 5.10a ★★   ❑

A good warm up for the area, although
it shares a lot of ground with the
following route. Climb the crack on
Abortion Control until the third bolt
where it is easy to transfer onto the face
proper, following jugs to the top.
Gear: 6 bolts   2-bolt anchor
FA: Alan Nelson, Richard Wright 1993

52 Abortion Control 5.8 ★★   ❑

Climb the obvious fist/offwidth crack
immediately right of *Bimbo in Limbo*.
Stay with the crack when *Bimbo* breaks
left onto the face, but use the anchors on
that route.
Gear: SR to #4 Camalot   shared anchor

Ben Schneider, *Bush Loves Detroit* (5.8), opposite page

North Quarry
← 1 mi

#85   #100   ⤹ Access Fund
Property Line

Broad
Gully

#150

#224
#212
Gully
#264
South Quarry
1mi
adlly

53 Killian's Red 5.11c ★★★

Start just right of the *Abortion Control* crack and climb up an easy face to the roof. Power through the undercling crux and breath easier on the jugs above. Continue motoring up flat edges and crimpers on the slightly slabby face above.
Gear: 6 bolts   2-bolt anchor
FA: Mike and Tom Carr 1991

54 Tanning Butter 5.11d ★★★

Stick clip the first bolt to protect the crux. Crank over a bulge and pull onto the low-angled blob above. Wander up the easier face above, staying on the skinny pillar between two crack systems just below the anchor.
Gear: 6 bolts   2-bolt anchor
FA: Alan Nelson 1998

Variation: Pass the Tanning Butter
5.10c ★★★ Because this bolted variation skips the short crux of the original route, it will probably be climbed more often as it makes for a more consistent route. Start to the left and climb past two bolts to join the original line at its third bolt *(7bolts). FA: Kirk Miller 2008*

55 Silver Bullet 5.10b ★★★

Interesting climbing up a slab that is broken up by a downward pointing block and a curving crack that leads into a small roof. Shoulder scum up a fin to the right of the roof, power over another roof, and take the slab to the anchor.
Gear: 9 bolts   2-bolt anchor
FA: Rick Leitner, Brian Hansen 1991

56 An Artichoke 5.10d ★★★

Start this great route on a bulge split by an irregular finger-sized crack. Continue into a dihedral and then to a prominent arête with interesting high steps and tiny, positive crimps.
Gear: 7 bolts   2-bolt anchor
FA: Richard Wright, Tod Anderson 1995

Variation: The Consolation 5.10a ★★★
Climb the original line to a ledge at the fourth bolt (10a). Break off right and follow a low-angled, right-facing dihedral to a ledge (5.8+), using the anchor on *Under the Wire. Gear: SR*

57 Under the Wire 5.10a ★★★

Begin immediately right of *An Artichoke* at twin cracks, which offer up first class climbing. Delicate moves above follow a line on a pillar that narrows and becomes freestanding at the top.
Gear: 4 bolts   2-bolt anchor
FA: Tod Anderson, Alan Nelson 1998

58 Generica 5.10b ★

This route is marked by the wide open book just off the ground with a clean left face. Stem the dihedral and follow a contrived line on the pillar above. Bear hugging the arête (5.10d) may have been the first ascentionist's original idea, but the sensible leader will clearly place a left foot on the narrow pillar to the left.
Gear: 6 bolts   2-bolt anchor
FA: Alan Nelson 1998

59 Left Side of Leaning Pillar (Fractions) 5.11a

As the name indicates, climb the left side of the pillar on the following route, eventually working out onto the arête and the anchors on *Back to the Bayou*.
Gear: 4 bolts   shared anchor
FA: Richard Wright 1997

35

North Quarry
← 1 mi

#85   #100 Access Fund
       Property Line

Broad
Gully

#150

60 Back to the Bayou 5.10c ★★ ❏
(Leaning Pillar)
Balance up the slender pillar just left of
the wide *Thin Lizzie* chimney. This route
originally sported just one bolt!
Gear: 6 bolts   2-bolt anchor
FA: Dave Hart, Pete Wisnie 1989

61 Thin Lizzie (Dodging Ions) 5.8 ❏
The name is a bit of a misnomer as
it begins in the corner underneath
a gaping chimney just right of the
preceding route. Work through
vegetation, avoid a bird's nest, and
move into the crack to the right of the
top of the chimney. Use the anchor on
Resolution.
Gear: SR   shared anchor

62 The Dissolution 5.11d ★★ ❏
A tad harder, but not as quality as its
sister climb *The Resolution*. The first bit of
hard climbing at the start can be avoided
by stemming onto the *Back to the Bayou*
pillar, as can the last difficult section near
the top of the chimney on *Thin Lizzie*.
That aside, the climbing is consistent and
difficult, with crimps that are a bit rough
on aging shoulders.
Gear: 7 bolts   shared anchor
FA: Tod Anderson, Richard Wright 1993

63 The Resolution 5.11c ★★★ ❏
Adjacent to *The Dissolution*, this route
is powerful from the first move. Tricky
labyacks, gastons and inobvious body
English will take the leader past a bulge
to good finger locks and a fun arête.
Gear: 6 bolts   2-bolt anchor
FA: Ken Trout, Guy Lords, Jim Garber 1992

64 Jell-O Brand Napalm 5.10b ★★ ❏
Begin around the corner from *The
Resolution* at a pair of discontinuous
cracks. Climb up jugs to the cracks and
make a difficult move to a locker hand
jam. Continue motoring up the face to
the top. Use the anchor on *The Resolution*
to descend.
Gear: SR   nearby anchor
FA: Richard and Scott Berk 1989

65 Big Rattler 5.8 ❏
Climb the broken dihedral just left of
Whole Lotta Drunk, using that anchor to
descend.
Gear: SR   nearby anchor

Derek Lawrence, *Crawling Up Roseanne's Belly* (5.11b), p. 32   photo: Jason Haas

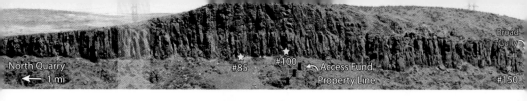

North Quarry
← 1 mi

#85　#100　⤴ Access Fund
Property Line

Broad Gully

#150

66 Whole Lotta Drunk 5.11a ★★ ☐
(Scott's a Vegetarian Now)

Named for the FAer's hangover prior to the ascent. This route ascends the clean face in the back of a shallow alcove 20ft right of *The Resolution*. Awkward and strenuous stemming takes the leader past the first bolt (stick clip if short) and up toward easier, wandering moves on the face above.

Gear: 6 bolts   2-bolt anchor
FA: Richard Wright, Joe Desimone 1996

THE TEN WORST TABLE ROUTES

So, you think you're a true Table local? Not until you've climbed the best of the best and…at least some of the worst of the worst. These ten routes should be avoided at all cost except by the truly deranged choss hunters.

① For Love of Mother Not 5.6 ■	⑥ Take Flight 5.10a ■
② Abortion Central 5.7 R ■	⑦ Uommama bin Rotten 5.10b X ■
③ Brieface Fulla Berries 5.7 ■	⑧ Unknown H 5.10c ■
④ POS Dihedral 5.8 ■	⑨ W.W.J.B. 5.10c ■
⑤ Dumb Politicians 5.10a ■	⑩ Table Manners 5.11c ■

THE AMERICAN ALPINE CLUB

SUPPORTING CLIMBERS SINCE 1902

www.AmericanAlpineClub.org

North Quarry
← 1 mi
#85   #100   Access Fund
Property Line
Broad Gully
#150

COLD SHUT/HOT SPOT AREA

Approach: While there is no clear separation, the area begins about 30ft right of *Whole Lotta Drunk*. There is also no clear separation in the cliff to help distinguish this area from Fence Area, although an easy scramble amongst the ledges just right of *Gold Shut Route* helps provide toprope access to a few of the routes.

67 Qualye Eats Bush 5.8+

Begin on the other side of a boulder, 20ft left of *Crowbar Cowboy*. Grunge up grubby rock for 30ft to a ledge, where the quality of the route quickly improves. Climb a right-facing corner to a slight overhang at the lip. Flop onto the top and belay on gear.
Gear: SR   walk off

68 Dumb Politicians 5.10a

This route is so bad the authors felt it didn't even warrant a description.
Gear: SR   walk off

Jon Haradon, *Crowbar Cowboy (5.9)*

69 Crowbar Cowboy 5.9 ★★★

This is an excellent route for leaders who want to safely push themselves at 5.9 or intro 5.11 on the variation. The route is marked by a clean triangular roof 30ft off the ground. Slopers on a bulbous arête lead to the roof (long draw). Make a committing move right to a jug and crank up the right side of the roof to the slab above.
Gear: 5 bolts   2-bolt anchor
FA: Deaun Schovajsa, Dave Gottenborg 1994
Variation: 5.11a ★★★ Pull over the roof directly instead of moving around it to the right.

70 A Quark for Quayle 5.9+

Begin at the base of the following route and follow a crack up into a corner system left of the bolts on *Crack and Face Route*. Pull into a short, hanging dihedral before finishing in a crumbly shoot. Traverse right to an anchor.
Gear: SR   shared anchor

71 Crack and Face Route 5.10c ★★★

Climb straight up to a slender pillar past a high first bolt and onto a ledge. This can be cheated with features on the right. Approach an airy second bolt on thin edges. From here, motor up to another ledge and finish out the slight overhang, which leads to the top.
Gear: 5 bolts   2-bolt anchor
FA: Tod Anderson, D. Field, E. Moskovics 1991

TOP FIFTEEN TABLE TRAD ROUTES

1. Killian's Dead 5.6 ■
2. Big Dihedral 5.8 ■
3. Bush Loves Detroit 5.8 ■
4. Fast Boat to China 5.8 ■
5. G-Spot 5.8 ■
6. Hand Crack 5.8 ■
7. Liar Liar 5.8 ■
8. Bad Manners 5.9 ■

9. The Short Tour 5.9 ■
10. Jell-O Brand Napalm 5.10b ■
11. Shadow of a Hangdog 5.10b ■
12. Burly Man 5.11a ■
13. Frank's Wild Years 5.11c ■
14. Silver Bullet 5.11d ■
15. Bone Crusher 5.12b ■

North Quarry
← 1 mi
#85 #100 ↶ Access Fund
Property Line
Broad
Gully
#150

72 Widespread Selfishness
5.12b ★★★
This sustained route takes the right side of the clean face just right of *Crack and Face Route*. Scamper past two easy bolts and then battle past sidepulls and technical feet. Move around to the right of a small roof and onto the slab above. May be hard for the grade.
Gear: 7 bolts   2-bolt anchor
FA: Ken Trout

73 The World Thru a Bottle
5.10a ★★
A clean, thin, right-facing corner begins above a chossy start and leads to an irregular crack that splits a beautiful streaked face.
Gear: SR   chain anchors

74 Honed to the Bone 5.8 ★
Not as wide as it looks, this crack begins in a left-facing corner and follows an arête to the right of the clean face split by *World Thru a Bottle*.
Gear: SR   shared anchor

75 Day of Reckoning 5.11d ★★★
Climb up easy rock to a ledge at the fourth bolt. Make a difficult fifth clip and follow sustained edges mixed with intermittent jugs to the top.
Gear: 8 bolts   2-bolt anchor
FA: Mark Rolofson, Kirk Miller 2008

76 Five to One 5.11a ★
Somewhat large moves on good holds lead up a smooth bolted slab eight feet right of the previous route. The lower face currently has lichen on it and could use a brush.
Gear: 8 bolts   2-bolt anchor
FA: Kirk Miller 2006

#224
#212
Gully
#264
South Quarry
1mi

77 Disappearing Man 5.10d ★★★ ❑

Start on the ledge above *Five to One* and *Nine to Five*. There is a single bolt anchor above the anchors on those two routes, which is better to belay from if doing this as a second pitch and not as an extension to *Five to One*. Monster holds appear exactly where they're needed on this gently overhanging face with exhilarating exposure. Currently hangers are missing on two of the bolts.

Gear: 5 bolts   chain anchor

78 Shut Down, Plugged Up, and Cold to Boot 5.7 ★ ❑

Start just left of the bolts on *Nine to Five* and climb up the semi-wide left-facing corner to the anchors on *Nine to Five*.

Gear: SR   shared anchor

Tony Milkus, *Nine to Five* (5.9), p. 44   photo: Ben Schneider

43

North Quarry
← 1 mi

#85   #100   Access Fund
                Property Line

Broad
Gully

#150

79 Nine to Five 5.9 ★★ ☐

This fun warm up is the next bolted line right of *Five to One*. Balance to the top of the pillar, then clip the anchor across the small gap.
Gear: 6 bolts   2-bolt anchor
FA: Alan Nelson 1996

⑧⓪ Mechanically Inept 5.8 ★ ☐

This is the quality crack sandwiched between *Nine to Five* and *Gold Shut Route*. Good jams lead to a shared anchor with *Gold Shut Route*.
Gear: SR   shared anchor

81 The Gold Shut Route 5.10a ★★ ☐

Start on the clean face just left of a jumbled fourth-class gully. The bolts seem to force this route to the left (11a), while the natural line follows easier ground just right of the bolts.
Gear: 3 bolts   2-bolt anchor

⑧② For Love of Mother Not 5.6 ☐

This horribly chossy right-facing corner begins above the previous two routes. Stem up soft rock, being careful not to cut too much loose in the process. Top out and use the anchors on *Disappearing Man*. There is a ring piton from the 1950s fixed in the lower part of the dihedral.
Gear: 1 fixed pin, SR   shared anchor

Fred Gravagna, *Killian's Red* (5.11c), p.35

FENCE AREA (BULGE AREA)

This is the tallest portion of the cliff and many of the routes require at least a 60meter rope, so read descriptions carefully. The wall is also west facing, soaking up late afternoon sun to make it one of the best walls for some after work cragging.

Approach: Begin 50ft right of *Gold Shut Route*. The area ends just beyond the Access Fund property line, where there is a stake in the ground next to *Electrocuticles*. This is virtually the only area that lacks convenient toprope access from above.

83 **NIMBY** 5.10a R ★ ❏
Start on a skinny pillar 25ft left of the following route. Hang on through the overhanging start past two bolts. From here, the face becomes lower-angled, but less protectable. Balance up the slab to the top (5.7 R). The third bolt was chopped.
Gear: 2 bolts, SR   2-bolt anchor
FA: Tod Anderson

84 Gruesome Groove 5.12a ★ ❏
(Pass the Basalt, Please)
Start immediately left of *Winter Warmer*. Climb into an awkward slot and solve the contorted crux at the first bolt. From the second bolt on, the route eases considerably, merging with *Winter Warmer Variation* at the roof. **60m rope.**
Gear: 11 bolts   shared anchor
FA: Keith Ainsworth 1997

85 Winter Warmer 5.10d ★★★ ❏
This route shares the start with the following route, but branches left at the second bolt. Move back right to tackle the right side of the overlap and finish on a juggy headwall before the anchor. The origianl line is shown in the yellow and black stripe on the photo. **60-meter rope required.**
Gear: 11 bolts   2-bolt anchor
FA: Dave Field, Ernie Moskovics 1993

86 Winter Warmer Variation ❏
5.10d ★★★
This route is a combination of the surrounding routes, but constitutes the best climbing out of the three. Climb *Winter Warmer* to the second bolt and then move right to join *Stickin' It to the Man* for a few bolts. At the roof, traverse left to the other side of it, merging with *Pass the Basalt Please* for the last few bolts below the anchor. **Use a 60m rope.**
Gear: 11 bolts   shared anchor

CLIMBERS, the **ENVIRONMENT** and **ACCESS**
are all connected
Know how you fit in. ▸▸

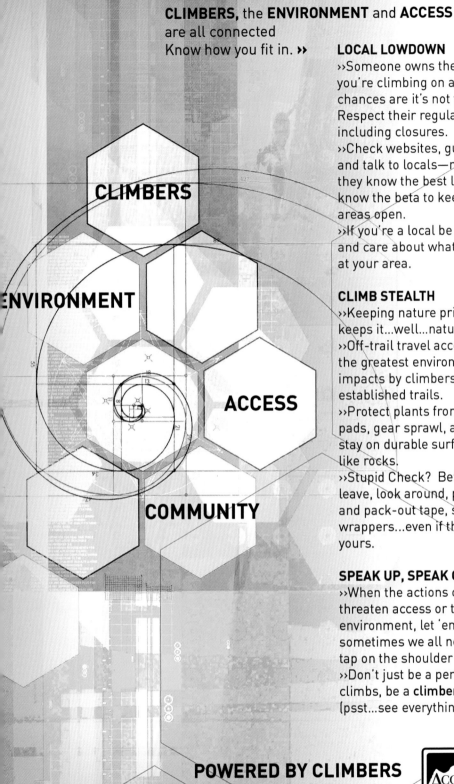

CLIMBERS

ENVIRONMENT

ACCESS

COMMUNITY

LOCAL LOWDOWN

▸▸Someone owns the land that you're climbing on and chances are it's not you. Respect their regulations, including closures.

▸▸Check websites, guidebooks, and talk to locals—not only do they know the best lines, they know the beta to keep the areas open.

▸▸If you're a local be informed and care about what happens at your area.

CLIMB STEALTH

▸▸Keeping nature pristine keeps it...well...natural.

▸▸Off-trail travel accounts for the greatest environmental impacts by climbers—stay on established trails.

▸▸Protect plants from packs, pads, gear sprawl, and feet; stay on durable surfaces—uh, like rocks.

▸▸Stupid Check? Before you leave, look around, pick-up and pack-out tape, spilt chalk, wrappers...even if they're not yours.

SPEAK UP, SPEAK OUT

▸▸When the actions of others threaten access or the environment, let 'em know-sometimes we all need a little tap on the shoulder

▸▸Don't just be a person who climbs, be a **climber** (psst...see everything above).

POWERED BY CLIMBERS
join at www.accessfund.org

ACCESS FUND

POWERED BY CLIMBERS

North Quarry
← 1 mi

#85 #100 Access Fund
Property Line

Broad
Gully

#150

87 Stickin' It to the Man 5.10a ★★★ ❑

Climb *Fenced In* for a few retro-bolts until it is possible to transfer onto a pedestal out left. Continue cranking up the juggy face as for *Winter Warmer Variation*, but at the top, stay right of the *Winter Warmer* roof. **Needs a 60-meter rope.**

Gear: 12 bolts   2-bolt anchor
FA: Tim Slater, Ken and Marsha Trout 2008

88 Fenced In 5.9 ★ ❑

Stem and jam up the large, tight-hands, right-facing corner immediately right of *Winter Warmer* to the ledge and anchors on *No Gumbies*. The start was retrobolted to make way for the previous route.

Gear: 3 bolts, SR   shared anchor

89 No Gumbies 10d ★ ❑

Begin in a large right-facing dihedral between *Ugly Stick* and *Stickin' It to the Man*. Climb up crack systems to gain a high bolt over a small, triangular roof. Climb the center of the slab on crisp edges to a definitive but well protected crux. When the slab ends, continue up the overhanging face to a pair of cold shuts just over a ledge. The route tries hard with questionable success to stay out of the crack on *Fenced In* and the chossy crack on the right.

Gear: 4 bolts, SR   2-bolt anchor
FA: Jim Burtle 1993

90 Ugly Stick 5.10b ★★★ ❑

At 120', this is the tallest route at Table and a 70meter rope is needed to get down with a single rope. An intermediate anchor was placed 40ft up for those with 50meter ropes to do two rappels. Begin 15ft right of *Winter Warmer* in an indistinct alcove. Layback up a right-facing flake for two bolts to the intermediate anchor. From here, continue up the pumpy face bolt after bolt, milking rests where possible to eventually gain the top of the cliff.

Gear: 16 bolts   3-bolt anchor
FA: Kirk Miller 2006

91 Crash Test Blondes 5.9 ★ ❑

This engaging layback begins 10ft left of and around the corner from *Basalt and Battery*. Surmount a small ledge and tackle a sharp layback. A blocky section leads to the anchor on *Basalt and Battery*.

Gear: SR   shared anchor

92 Basalt and Battery 5.10c ★★★ ❑

This is an unusual route for Table, with hard moves leading to the first bolt. Awkward and somewhat humorous moves follow, which may indeed batter the unprepared leader.

Gear: 7 bolts   2-bolt anchor
FA: Dave Field, Ernie Moskovics

93 Insult and Flattery 5.12a ★★ ❑

This is the second pitch of *Basalt and Battery*. From the 2-bolt anchor atop that route, a reachy first bolt just over a small, mossy roof protects the crux. From here, fun, steep climbing gives way to easier ground before the anchor. Make one rappel with a single 60meter rope or two raps with a 50meter.

Gear: 4 bolts   2-bolt anchor
FA: Tod Anderson

94 At Fault for Chattery 5.10b ★★★ ❑
Begin in the gray nook just right of *Basalt and Battery*. Climb the inset, stretching out left to the high first bolt. Continue stemming, gradually transferring to the arête on the left at the second bolt to enjoy positive holds and interesting moves. Merge with *Basalt and Battery* at that route's sixth bolt.
Gear: 5 bolts   shared anchor
FA: Tod Anderson

95 Klimbink is Ferbolten 5.11d ★★ ❑
Because of the landing, a stick clip for the second bolt may be a good idea. Slap up the arête on sloping sidepulls and edges to easier ground above the second bolt.
Gear: 8 bolts   2-bolt anchor
FA: Guy Lords, Ken Trout

96 F.A.T.A.L. 5.10b ★★★　　❑
Stellar, thought provoking climbing in the deep dihedral just right of *Klimbink*. Stem up the obtuse corner as your "Femurs And Tibias Alternate Laterally".
Gear: 4 bolts   2-bolt anchor

97 Electrocuticles 5.12a ★★　❑
This route begins behind the fence line marking the end of the Access Fund's property line immediately right of *F.A.T.A.L.* Climb positive features to thin crimps which clearly tell climbers how the route was named.
Gear: 5 bolts   2-bolt anchor
FA: Ken Trout, Rick Leitner

Jon Haradon, *F.A.T.A.L.* (5.10b)   photo: Jason Haas

98 Foul Play 5.9 ★　　　　❑
Begin 10ft right of *Electrocuticles* and climb up into a short, shallow chimney. At the top of it, break left into a positive layback leading to a ledge. Move left to the *Electrocuticles* anchor.
Gear: SR to #5 Camalot   shared anchor

99 POS Dihedral 5.8　　　　❑
Begin immediately left of *Solar Panel* and climb up broken, lichen covered, loose dihedrals to a decaying webbing anchor around a horn and bail (5.7), or continue up a crack for another 15ft and traverse right to the anchor on *Solar Panel*. Because of the broken nature of the route, several variations of similar difficulty exist for both the bottom and top half.
Gear: SR   webbing anchor

Geoff Elson, *Solar Panel* (5.12d), p. 52

photo: Jason Haas

North Quarry
← 1 mi
#85   #100   Access Fund
Property Line
Broad Gully
#150

100 Solar Panel 5.12d ★★ ❑

This esthetically smooth headwall is the hardest route at Table and appears to be devoid of any holds whatsoever when viewed from the ground. Scuttle up an open book and then move out onto the smooth face at the first bolt. Master the dance of precision footwork with powerful lock offs over the roof and catch a welcomed rest above the third bolt. Move out to the right arête and slap up to the sloping finish.
Gear: 5 bolts   Coldshut anchors
FA: Mark Rolofson 1993

101 G-Spot 5.8 ★★★ ❑

Unobvious moves make you think, while at the same time the difficulty never exceeds 5.8, making this a great trad route by Table Mountain standards. Start just right of *Solar Panel* and climb up a discontinuous crack system to a small roof with a bolt. Transition slightly right over the roof and climb a crack as for *Power of Tower* to the same anchor.
Gear: 1 bolt, SR   shared anchor

102 Power of Tower 5.11b R ★★ ❑

Start underneath a small, triangular roof 20ft right of *Solar Panel*. Boulder up a face to a high bolt below the roof (5.9 R), solve the technical roof to clip another bolt before pulling onto a slab. Motor up the slab with a crack on the left to chain anchors.
Gear: 2 bolts, SR   bolted anchor

103 Abortion Central 5.7 R ❑

The name says it all, as few will finish leading this route if they are crazy enough to try to in the first place. Stem up an inset with unconsolidated rock to a ledge. Work up a vibrating pillar to another ledge near the anchor on *Power of Tower*. Continue up broken and poorly protected rock to the top of the cliff.
Gear: SR to #4 Camalot   walk off
FA: Dave Hart, Richard Berk 1987

104 Slot to Trot 5.9 ★ ❑

Climb a finger crack in a right-facing dihedral immediately left of *Unknown H* to a ledge. From here, climb a bolted face to an anchor.
Gear: 5 bolts, SR   2-bolt anchor
FA: Kirk Miller 2007

105 Unknown H 5.10c ❑

Locate a bolted route just before a scruffy section of cliff leading to the Twelve Pack Wall. Climb up a sketchy, hollow-sounding flake to the right of the first bolt. Traverse hard left at the third bolt to a tight finger crack. Protect out a hand crack to the left and continue up and back right to the top of the wall. This route has a useless fourth bolt way right of the plumb line and could stand to be re-engineered.
Gear: 5 bolts, hand-sized cam   2-bolt anchor

North Quarry
← 1 mi

#85

#100

Access Fund
Property Line

Broad
Gully

#150

TWELVE PACK WALL

Approach: Walk 300ft right from Fence Area, past a broken, unattractive portion of the cliff line. The area ends at a grubby, low fifth class, right-facing dihedral about 30ft left of *Scarlett's Pulse*, which serves as a divider between Twelve Pack Wall and Industrial Buttress. If setting up a toprope, it is advised to walk up the gully on the right side of Industrial Buttress instead of this gully.

106 C'est le Morte 5.8

Start as for the following route, but quickly trend left and climb a face to the left of the *Briefcase Fulla Blues* roof. A clean dihedral above a juggy roof then leads to a stance, joining back up with the previous route for the last five feet.
Gear: SR   walk off

107 Briefcase Fulla Blues 5.7

Rarely does a route climb worse than it looks. Loose blocks, hollow flakes, and a rocky sandbox waiting to avalanche off the top make this such a route. Begin left of the previous route underneath a triangular roof and follow a deep crack past the roof, up a dihedral and on to a loose summit. Belay on gear.
Gear: SR   walk off

108 Psycho Beta Buck Down
5.12a ★

Climb a slab to a small crux overhang. Navigate the tricky sequence to a low-angled section and a pair of cold shuts.
Gear: 4 bolts   bolted anchor

109 Unknown I 5.10b ★★★

Begin on the left arête of the following route's dihedral. This excellent climb offers several variations down low. Slap up the arête, step into the discontinuous crack on the right, and then climb past the roof on *Raw Fish and Rice*. Follow the bolts to the top.
Gear: 6 bolts   2-bolt anchor

110 Raw Fish and Rice 5.10b ★★

Climb up a low-angled crack in a right-facing dihedral between the bolts on *Unknown I* and *Unknown J*. Surmount the white streaked roof via awkward fingers, with a juggy crack above leading to the anchors on *Unknown J*.
Gear: SR   shared anchor
FA: Scott and Richard Berk 1986

111 Unknown J 5.9 ★

This contrived route tackles the right side of a large roof immediately right of the preceding route. Climb up a slab to the roof and choose to take it head on for a very difficult feat, or slightly to the side at 5.9, or to the way right in an easy corner for 5.6. Continue up the face for a few more bolts to the top.
Gear: 8 bolts   2-bolt anchor

112 Honey, I Shrunk the Hemorrhoids 5.7 ★★★

Start just right of the preceding route and pull through a balancy, reachy crux start to gain a lower-angled section that leads to a narrow pinnacle. Catch a rest and then balance up the bolted arête to the anchors. New or tentative leaders may want gear to one inch to compensate for the space between the initial few bolts. While hardley anyone ever brings gear on this route, it is R-rated over moderate terrain if no supplemental gear is used.
Gear: 4 bolts   2-bolt anchor
FA: Deaun Schovajsa, Dave Gottenborg 1994

North Quarry
← 1 mi
#85 #100 ↖ Access Fund
Property Line
Broad Gully
#150

113 Love, Sex, and the IRS 5.8 ★ ❑
Climb a crack in a left-facing corner just left of *Chunky Monkey*. Pull through a slot to join *Chunky Monkey* at the fifth bolt.
Gear: 2 bolts, SR   2-bolt anchor
FA: Richard and Scott Berk 1987

114 Chunky Monkey 5.10b ★★ ❑
Begin on the obvious flat prow. Follow the bolts over a bulge and onto a ledge before continuing up a headwall.
Gear: 7 bolts   2-bolt anchor

115 Spit Fires and Funeral Parlours 5.9 ★ ❑
Start on the face immediately right of the bolts on *Chunky Monkey*. Boulder up the face, placing thin gear, to a ledge. Traverse left to merge with *Chunky Monkey* at its fifth bolt.
Gear: 2 bolts, SR   2-bolt anchor
FA: R. Berk, Dave Hart, Ryan Nassimbene 1987

116 Pump You Up 5.9- ❑
Jam up a crack to the left of the double cracks on *Unknown K* as it arcs right to meet at the bulge of *Unknown K*. Climb a crack to the left of the bulge and finish with a hand crack just left of the finish for the following route.
Gear: SR   walk off

117 Unknown K 5.8 ❑
Located in an open book just right of *Pump You Up* that's bound by double cracks. Stay right past the bulge and follow a thin seam and chossy blocks to a natural anchor.
Gear: SR   walk off

118 See You, See Me 5.6 ❑
Begin 10ft right of the previous route in a fifth class descent gully/inset between Twelve Pack Wall and Industrial Buttress. Angle right to a right-leaning hand crack that runs up to the right of a small roof. Finish on a clean face above the obvious roof. Belay on gear.
Gear: SR   walk off

Christine Hill, *Honey I Shrank the Hemorrhoids* (5.7), p. 54   photo: Jason Haas

North Quarry
← 1 mi
#85
#100
Access Fund
Property Line
#150
Broad
Gully

INDUSTRIAL BUTTRESS

Approach: Walk right of a grubby, low fifth class, right-facing dihedral that is about 30ft left of *Scarlett's Pulse*. At the right end of the wall, there is a 15ft wide corridor/gully separating Industrial Buttress from the MBA Area, which allows easy toprope access to nearby routes for both areas. The area is also easily identified by two large white "67"s painted on the rock. The blocky gully on the left side, separating Industrial Buttress from Twelve Pack Wall should not be used for toproping access as it is harder and not as safe as the gully on the right.

119 Scarlett's Pulse 5.7

Start 30ft left of *Politicians* at a seven-foot boulder blocking access to a large open book. Scramble up the V-shaped groove, through a short, thin-crack layback and up to a wide flake on the left. Layback up the resonating flake, asking if all that wide gear will actually hold. Belay on gear and scramble down a gully to the right, which marks the end of the Industrial Buttress.
Gear: SR to #5 Camalot   walk off

120 Belly Up 5.6

Perhaps this route earned its name because this is the position in which you could find yourself if just one of the many loose blocks ripped loose and sent you to the bottom. Climb a long 4th class gully to a short, dirty, loose slot with a crack on the left wall. Use the anchors on *Heidi Hi*.
Gear: SR   nearby anchor

121 Heidi Hi 5.8 ★★

Climb the following route to a ledge atop the inset. Step left into the obvious splitter and juggy crack. Finish in a V-shaped groove.
Gear: SR   2-bolt anchor
FA: Ryan Nassimbene, Dave Sams 1987
Variation: Toure Koundra 5.7 This is listed for historical reasons, not as a suggestion to climb it. Begin around to the left of the inset as for *Heidi Hi* and climb a crack next to a boulder. Reach the ledge directly below the upper crack and finish with the normal route.

122 Politicians, Priests, and Body Bags 5.10a ★★

Begin in a four-foot wide inset with a high quality hand crack on the right or good fingers in the left corner. From the top of the inset, step into the crack on the right and follow the bolts on the left.
Gear: 4 bolts, SR   2-bolt anchor
FA: Richard Berk, Dave Hart 1987

Ben Schneider, *Feeding Frenzy* (5.11d), p.64

photo: Jason Haas

125 Noodle Factory 5.9 ★★★ ❑

Begin three feet right of *Fast Boat to China* at a crack in a shallow open book. Follow crack systems up to a ledge in a deep open book and to the left of a headwall. Merge with *Fast Boat* for 20ft and then branch off to the right to finish with an overhanging hand crack.
Gear: SR shared anchor
FA: Dave Hart 1988

126 Salad Bar 5.10a ★★ ❑

The last book mislabeled this as *The John Roskelly Show*, which is actually route 129. Move five feet right of *Noodle Factory* to a stubby right-facing dihedral. Work up the corner to a V-shaped crack and a bolt. Transition right into a crack and jam to a ledge. Follow the heavily featured face past two more bolts, supplementing with gear, to the top.
Gear: 3 bolts, SR 2-bolt anchor
FA: Jeff Brown, Dave Hart, Richard Berk 1988

127 Nipple Phyle 5.6 ❑

Low-angled jumbled blocks give way to a flared and shallow crack just right of *Salad Bar*. Set a directional up top and lower off the anchors on *Salad Bar*.
Gear: SR nearby anchor
FA: B. Asbury, Dave Hart 1988

128 Left-Hand Monkey Wrench 5.7 ❑

Start just right of *Nipple Phyle* and mantle past a series of low-angled, excrement smeared ledges to a hand crack finish. Traverse left to the anchor on *Salad Bar* to descend.
Gear: SR to #3.5 Camalot nearby anchor
FA: Dave Hart, B. Asbury 1988

123 W.W.J.B. 5.10c ❑

What Would Jesus Bolt? Hopefully not this squeeze job, which shares the thin strip of real estate between the previous route and *Fast Boat to China*. Careful not to grab the wrong holds or you'll be cheating with *Politicians*. This should have been left as a toprope variation.
Gear: 6 bolts shared anchor

124 Fast Boat to China 5.8 ★★★ ❑

Jam a short, slightly overhanging, right-facing corner to a ledge. A finger crack in the dihedral leads to another ledge. Merge with *Noodle Factory* for 20ft and then take the left-hand finish through double cracks in a corner.
Gear: SR 2-bolt anchor
FA: Scott Berk solo 1986

Laramie Duncan, *Industrial Disease* (5.11c), p.62

Broad
Gully

North Quarry
← 1 mi
#85   #100   ↰ Access Fund
Property Line
#150

129 **The John Roskelly Show**
(Polyvinyl Chloride) 5.9+ ★ ❏
A few jumbled blocks at the base of this
right-facing corner lead into a clean,
thin, hanging dihedral. Stem up to
the top and lower off the anchors on
Take Flight. This is not a good route for
leaders at their limit.
Gear: SR   shared anchor
FA: Dave Hart 1987

130 **Take Flight** 5.10a   ❏
Located approximately 11inches
left of *Blow Chow*, this line defines
the word contrived. Even trying to
climb independently of the previous
route and *Blow Chow* is an exercise in
ridiculousness. Boycott bad bolting and
don't climb this route.
Gear: 7 bolts   2-bolt anchor

131 **Blow Chow** 5.8 ★★   ❏
Find a wavy crack immediately left of
Flight 67. Alternate between offwidth
pods and deep hand jams in what
appears to be a chimney, slithering up to
the anchors on the previous route.
Gear: SR to #4 Camalot   shared anchor

132 **Flight 67 to**
Stockholm 5.11a ★★   ❏
Climb the left side of the overhanging
Industrial Disease headwall, starting
directly beneath a fading "67" 8ft up.
Gear: 8 bolts   2-bolt anchor
FA: Richard and Scott Berk, Dave Hart 1988

133 **Industrial Disease** 5.11c ★★★   ❏
(Dead Moonies Don't Sell Flowers)
This route is high quality and full value
from beginning to end. Easy climbing
leads to a high first bolt and then
delicately follows a balancy thin seam to
a horizontal break below an overhang.
Gain the headwall and try to hang on 'til
the end.
Gear: 7 bolts   2-bolt anchor
FA: Tod Anderson, Dave Field, Richard Wright

134 **Forgotten Names** 5.11d ★   ❏
Climb *Darker is Better* to the ledge next
to the "67". Step left onto an obvious
bolted headwall, using the thin seam
and left-hand arête to gain the chains.
Gear: 4 bolts, SR   chain anchors
FA: Richard Wright, Tod Anderson 1995

135 **Darker is Better** 5.7 ★★   ❏
This double crack corner begins directly
below the white painted streaks left by
the class of '67 enginerds. Solid jams
and jugs lead past the "67" and into the
sinker crack on the right. Top out and
belay on gear. Scramble down the gulley
to the right.
Gear: SR to #3.5 Camalot (for anchor)   Walk off
Variation: Thunderbird (Light Beer) 5.8-
From the block atop the "67", climb
straight up into the chossy crack to the
left of the main line.

136 **Top Rope Face One** 5.8 TR ★   ❏
This toprope shares a natural anchor
with *Darker is Better*, but is located on
the backside of the painted "67". Jams in
a slot lead up an arête and over blocky
ledges to the top.

North Quarry
← 1 mi
#85   #100   Access Fund
Property Line
Broad
Gully
#150

MBA AREA (FIRST CRAG)

Approach: Walk 80ft right from *Darker is Better* and the painted "67" to the bolts on *Cliff Hanger*, with the towers between too short and blocky to bother bolting. For toproping, the broad gully on the right end of the wall allows easy TR access for routes at both MBA and Overhang Area, as does the gully to the left of *Cliff Hanger*.

137 Cliff Hanger 5.9+ ★   ❏
Start just left of the *Adrenalyzer* boulder and surmount a two-bolt slab, scrambling up a vegetated ledge to an obvious arête. The climbing stays far left of the bolts, which seem to try and force the line onto the arête.
Gear: 6 bolts   2-bolt anchor
FA: Alan Nelson 2001

138 Sick Minds Think Alike 5.8 ★   ❏
Solid jams ascend this obvious crack between the bolts on *Cliff Hanger* and *Spike*. Top out and clip either of those two routes' anchors.
Gear: SR   shared anchor

139 Adrenalyzer V1 ★★★   ❏
Just left of *Spike* is a 25ft, triangular shaped boulder. Climb the south face up the right-hand arête, avoiding moving too far left to inconsequential terrain.

140 Spike 5.10b ★★★   ❏
Find a bolted line between the *Adrenalyzer* and *Fatal Attraction* boulders. Balance up the crimpy face taking great care not to knock the namesake "spike" boulder cantilevered on a ledge at mid-height.
Gear: 6 bolts   2-bolt anchor
FA: Alan Nelson 2001

141 Fatal Attraction V1   ❏
Locate a pointed, left-angling boulder right of *Spike*. Start on a pedestal amongst some shrubs and climb left-angling jugs to the top. Tall people can virtually skip the entire route, detracting any redeeming qualities it may possess.

142 Brain Dead Ted 5.8 R   ❏
Start immediately left of the following route and behind the previous boulder problem. Climb up the indistinct, blocky, unprotected face to the top and belay on gear. Rappel from *Spike*.
Gear: SR   nearby anchor

143 How Retrobolting 5.7   ❏
Chimney up the slot immediately left of *Feeding Frenzy*. Rap from the anchors on that route.
Gear: SR to #5 Camalot   shared anchor

144 Feeding Frenzy 5.11d ★★★   ❏
This route marked the explosion of route development at Table as the secret was finally out. Climb a slab, scooting around to a large, hanging left-facing dihedral. Move off a narrow shelf and get into the thin, technical corner. The smearing finish up the dihedral will keep your attention to the very end.
Gear: 7 bolts   2-bolt anchor
FA: Tod Anderson, Dave Field, R. Wright 1993

North Quarry
← 1 mi
#85 #100 ↰ Access Fund
Property Line
Broad
Gully
#150

145 Shark Infested Waters (Shark Attack) 5.10d ★★

Climb *Feeding Frenzy* to the third bolt and then break off to the right into an overhanging, right-facing corner. Rappel from anchor on *Feeding Frenzy*.
Gear: 3 bolts, SR   shared anchor
FA: Tod Anderson

146 Mournful Mullet 5.8

This starts as a hand crack between the bolts on *Feeding Frenzy* and the following route. Jam over a small roof halfway up the route and then grovel up a featured chimney that tightens towards the top.
Gear: SR to #5 Camalot

147 Major Bolt Achievement 5.11a ★★★

This quality route starts a few feet right of the obvious *Feeding Frenzy* dihedral. Crimp past the bolts, staying out of the *Mournful Mullet* slot halfway up. Pull a wild roof just before the anchor.
Gear: 7 bolts   2-bolt anchor
FA: Tod Anderson, R. Wright, Dave Field 1993

148 Mandela (Leaning Pillar) 5.7 ★

This is the clean lieback corner on the left side of the *Brain Cloud* arête, with which it shares anchors.
Gear: SR   shared anchor
FA: Dave Hart, Richard Berk 1990

149 Brain Cloud 5.9 ★★★ (Shadow Arete)

Climb the stellar arête right of *Major Bolt Achievement*.
Gear: 5 bolts   chain anchors
FA: Ed Eash et al. 1992

150 Shadow of a Hangdog (Fat Fingers) 5.10b ★★★

Start just right of the *Brain Cloud* arête. Climb a crack that angles up and right to an off-fingers splitter at two-thirds height. Lay it back or climb the splitter head on, although despite the route also being known as *Fat Fingers*, it is doubtful that even chubby fingers will be able to finger lock the crack. Gain a ledge with bolted anchors.
Gear: SR   2-bolt anchor
FA: Scott and Richard Berk, Dave Hart 1987

151 Broken Arrow 5.11c ★

Begin a few feet right of the previous route. Climb up and right through a crack system to a small bulge. Crimp past three bolts (crux), avoiding the stem out to the *Stoney Middleton* corner. Use the anchors on the previous route.
Gear: 3 bolts, SR   shared anchors
FA: Dan Hare, Claire Mearns 2000

152 Stoney Middleton 5.8 ★★

This right-facing corner is just left of the smooth face on *Table Manners*. Work up to a ledge with anchors for *Shadow of a Hangdog* and bail out, or continue to the top of the cliff and walk off.
Gear: SR   walk off

Mike Cichon, *Shadow of a Hangdog* (5.10b), opposite page

153 Table Manners 5.11c ☐

Heavily contrived. The smooth, blank face that contains the bolts has no usable holds, while the crack to the right that climbers actually use takes great gear and is listed as the following route, *Bad Manners*. Climb the crack to the second bolt before doing a contrived traverse left, then back right after another bolt to the original crack on *Bad Manners*. Most will also pull the roof on the left, which coincidently accepts gear and is also an easier sequence.
Gear: 6 bolts   2-bolt anchor

154 Bad Manners 5.9 ★★★ ☐

This is the trad version of *Table Manners*. Climb the left-facing dihedral to the roof, pulling over it on the left side. Top out or clip the anchors on *Table Manners* to the right.
Gear: SR   shared anchor

155 Restless Heart 5.11b ★ ☐

This sport route is best identified by its black hangers and is the first sport route to the right of *Table Manners*. Climb a few discontinuous arêtes to a wide slot just right of a large roof. Shares anchors with *Table Manners*.
Gear: 7 bolts   shared anchor
FA: Mo Hershoff, Jim Erickson, Dan Hare 2001
Variation: 5.11d ★ Tackle the roof at the top instead of moving into the chimney.

156 Unknown L 5.8 ★ ☐

Climb a left-facing dihedral immediately left of *Good Man Dan*, using the anchor on that line.
Gear: SR   shared anchor

157 Good Man Dan 5.9+ ★★ ☐

This is the bolted arête just before the cliff makes a small bend to the east. Balance past several bolts to a ledge before finishing on the face above.
Gear: 7 bolts   2-bolt anchor
FA: Alan Nelson 2001

158 Unknown M 5.9- ★ ☐

Climb a crack in a shallow right-facing dihedral just right of *Good Man Dan*. There is a single bolt to protect the runout just before the anchor at the top.
Gear: 1 bolt, SR   bolted anchor

159 Unknown N 5.10c ★ ☐

This bolted face is around the corner to the right of *Good Man Dan* on an east-facing wall. Climb past the first bolt to a ledge, then tackle an awkward crux in a narrow boxy slot at the second bolt. Continue up the face to a bolted anchor.
Gear: 5 bolts   2-bolt anchor

160 Hodat? 5.9- ☐

Climb a left-facing dihedral a few feet right of the previous route. Top out and rap from anchors on *Unknown N*.
Gear: SR   shared anchor

161 Wazup? 5.8+ ★ ☐

This trad route climbs the left-facing pinnacle right of *Hodat?* Climb the right crack as it turns into a left-facing dihedral. Rap from anchors on a ledge.
Gear: SR   2-bolt anchor

162 The Mini Me 5.11b ★ ☐

This route may be short, but it sure is burly and is the last bolted line before the cliff breaks down into a gully separating the MBA and Overhang Areas. Avoid using the *Wazup?* crack.
Gear: 3 bolts   2-bolt anchor
FA: Dan Hare, Jonathan Degenhart 2000

South Quarry
1mi →

North Quarry
← 1 mi

#85   #100   ↖ Access Fund
Property Line

Broad
Gully

#150

OVERHANG AREA (SECOND CRAG)

Approach: Walk right across the broad gully from *The Mini Me* to where the cliff picks up again. However, there is no clear distinction about where Overhang Area ends and where Brown Cloud Crags begins aside from the fact that Overhang Area is considered to end right where the approach trail from the parking lot reaches the base of the main cliff at *This Ain't Naturita Pilgrim*. Also, the name is a bit of a misnomer because there are no real overhangs here, although there are a few short roofs and faces that approach 95 degrees. Routes 163-180 are sometimes referred to as the Trad Lands.

163 Passerby V0- ★

Begin 30ft left of *Little Ox* around the corner and up the gully. This is the first pillar after the cliff picks back up again after the broad gully separating the MBA and Overhang Areas. Climb the center of the 12ft soda can to a flat top out.

164 Little Ox 5.7 ★

Approach this route from either side of a large semi-detached block just left of *Big O' Flyer*. Climb the arête above the "OX" graffiti.
Gear: 3 bolts   2-bolt anchor
FA: Alan Nelson 2001

165 Oxymoron 5.6

Climb the crack between *Little Ox* and *Big O' Flyer*. Use gear or clip the first two bolts on *Little Ox*. Top-out at either anchor.
Gear: SR   shared anchor

166 Big O' Flyer 5.7 ★

Begin by jamming a small overhang in a right-facing nook. Move up a clean face past two large ledges. Rappel or walk off to the left to avoid potentially jamming the rope in a groove.
Gear: 4 bolts   2-bolt anchor
FA: Alan Nelson 2001

167 Line it Up 5.7 ★

Climb the crack just right of *Big O' Flyer*. Top out and descend from any of the nearby anchors.
Gear: SR   nearby anchor

168 X It 5.10a ★★

Climb the face past three bolts to a left-facing dihedral capped by a triangular roof. Pull the roof and finish on the face above.
Gear: 5 bolts   2-bolt anchor
FA: Alan Nelson 2001

169 Startled 5.8 ★

Move eight feet right of *X It*. Boulder up through the crux start to gain the first bolt and continue to the top of the block, transitioning left to join *X It* at the last bolt.
Gear: 5 bolts   shared anchor
FA: Alan Nelson 2001

170 Liar Liar 5.8 ★★★

This trad line starts immediately right of *Startled* in a shallow, blocky corner. Trend right onto a stance and climb a clean juggy crack into a great right-facing corner.
Gear: SR   2-bolt anchor
Variation: 5.8 Start in a shallow groove a few feet left of the main line and climb a deep slot to the same anchor.

171 Resident Bush 5.9 ★★

Begin 15ft right of *Startled*. Climb a rounded prow to a ledge. Move right to finish on the face above.
Gear: 6 bolts   2-bolt anchor
FA: Alan Nelson 2001

172 Traditions 5.10a ★★

Climb *Resident Bush* to the second bolt and then move right into a right-facing dihedral and crack system. Move out underneath a small roof and continue up to the anchors on *Resident Bush*.
Gear: 2 bolts, SR   shared anchor

173 Chopless 5.8 ★

Start on the left side of an amorphous blob and climb clean, changing-corners to a ledge. Move left to the *Resident Bush* anchors.
Gear: SR   shared anchor

174 Corn Flakes 5.8+ R ★

Begin halfway between *Resident Bush* and *BM Route* on a low-angled, amorphous boulder heap. Scramble up a gully to the base of a five-foot tall, hollow, dagger-like flake. Gingerly work past the flake, up the face, and into a right-facing dihedral, merging with the end of *Chopless* near a ledge.
Gear: SR   shared anchor

175 BM Route 5.9+ ★

Begin 50ft right of *Resident Bush* on the engraved "BM" arête. Climb the left side of the arête, avoiding scraping your back on the back wall.
Gear: 5 bolts   2-bolt anchor
Variation: 5.8 ★ Climb the right side of the arête as for *BM Route* using gear. This fell down in April 2008!

176 Tootsie Roll 5.8 ★★

Scale the featured face that resembles Tootsie Rolls 10ft left of the smooth rock on *Under the Table*.
Gear: 3 bolts   2-bolt anchor

177 Under the Table 5.11b ★★★

This face, resembling something in a quarry, became much more difficult when the wall literally collapsed and is now strewn about the base of the cliff, leaving a smooth face that has since been rebolted. This new and improved route is intended to follow a plum line near the bolts, but can be made easier by cheating out right on the arête.
Gear: 5 bolts   2-bolt anchor
FA: Mo Hershoff, Claire Mearns, D. Hare 1999

178 Alan's Seam 5.10a ★★

Climb a bolted left-slanting crack to a small roof. Crank over the bulge and move right on the ledge to the anchors above *Meat is Murder*.
Gear: 5 bolts   shared anchor
FA: Alan Nelson 2001

179 Meat is Murder 5.8 ★★

Climb a combination of two cracks near the small *Mindless* pillar, mostly using wide-hands or tight fists.
Gear: SR to #4 Camalot   2-bolt anchor
FA: Scott Berk, Dave Hart 1987
Variation: 5.10a ★ Climb only the thinner, left crack.

North Quarry
← 1 mi

#85   #100   ↰ Access Fund
Property Line

Broad Gully

#150

Joe Chorny, *Under the Table* (5.11b), p. 72

⟨180⟩ Mindless V0 ★

Boulder up a stubby pinnacle that sits in front of *Meat is Murder* and *Mind Mantle Arête*. It may be worth doing if you find yourself being the odd man out, sitting around waiting for a belay. Originally done as the direct start to *Meat is Murder*.

181 Mind Mantle Arête 5.11a ★★

Move around the right side of a pillar next to *Meat is Murder* to an arête with an east-facing bolt line. Climb the arête proper, staying belly-to-the-bolts and see why the crux gave this route its name. It is possible to also climb the crack and face to the right of the arête, clipping the same bolts and making the route only 5.10a.
Gear: 5 bolts   2-bolt anchor

⟨182⟩ 69.5 Crack 5.8 ★

Begin 10ft left of *Table Top* and angle up and right via a hand-and-finger crack. Stemming out wide on the left wall will slightly lessen the difficulty. Top out and rappel from the anchors on *Table Top*.
Gear: SR   shared anchor
FA: Randy & Belen Carmichael, P. Cogan 2005

183 Table Top 5.10c ★★

Climb a prominent pillar 25ft right of *Mind Mantle Arête*. A hand-sized cam is helpful below the high first bolt.
Gear: 4 bolts   2-bolt anchor
FA: Tod Anderson, Dave Field

184 Kevin Spies the Line 5.6 ★★★

Move 30ft right of *Table Top* and be prepared to take a number in order to get on this popular route. Climb a tricky start through the first bolt and enjoy casual jugs to gain rappel hangers, which should be rappelled from, as lowering through them will severely kink the rope.
Gear: 5 bolts   2-bolt anchor

⟨185⟩ Kevin's Trad Line 5.7 ★

Pick your way through broken crack systems on the slab just right of the previous route, protecting on gear. Build an anchor and walk off
Gear: SR   walk off

⟨186⟩ Redrum 5.7 ★★

Climb a chimney with a hand crack in it 15ft left of *Henry Spies the Line* and rappel from the anchors on that route.
Gear: SR   shared anchor

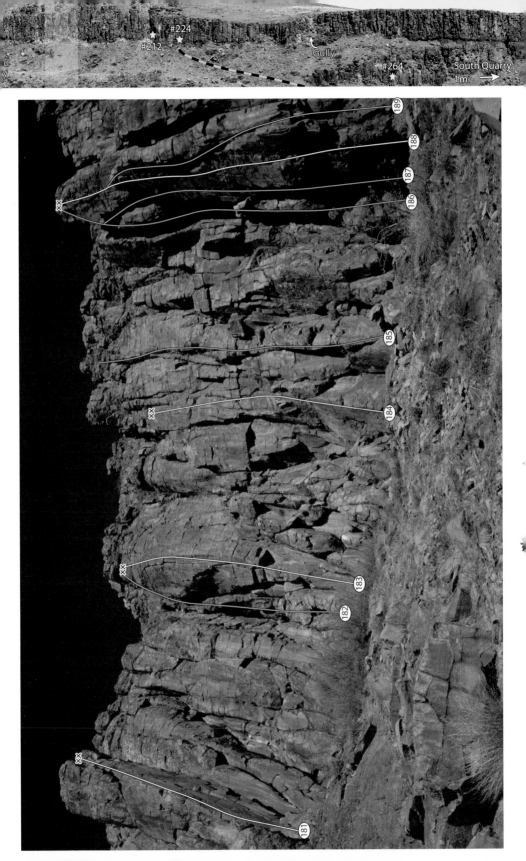

North Quarry
← 1 mi

#85 #100 Access Fund
Property Line

Broad
Gully

#150

187 Sleeper 5.8 ★

Start near a large block a few feet left of the following route. Climb discontinuous crack and ledge systems to top out on a pillar just down and left of the anchors on *Henry Spies the Line*.
Gear: SR   shared anchor

188 Henry Spies the Line (Franklin's Tower) 5.10a ★★★

Located on the west face just left of an arête, 50ft right of *Kevin Spies the Line*. There is a short crux after the first bolt.
Gear: 5 bolts   2-bolt anchor
FA: Dennis McCarin

189 Let's Wake up Ronnie and Barb 5.9- ★

Climb the crack on the right side of the arête as for the previous sport route until it switches sides. Stay in the crack, avoiding the upper half of *Henry Spies*.
Gear: SR   bolted anchor

190 Drinking Wine with the Chinese 5.9 ★★

Start at the base of *Death of Innocents* and move up and left into a shallow corner system. Jam up the crack with hands and perfect fingers to the anchors on *Death of Innocents*. While the route takes perfect gear, you can reach out right to clip the bolts on *Death of Innocents*.
Gear: SR   shared anchor

191 Death of Innocents 5.11b ★★ (Hug the Butt)

Start by underclinging a shark's tooth-like feature 10ft right of *Henry Spies the Line* at the first sport route after the wall curves back around a corner. Jam a crack, crimp the face, and then slap up the arête to the anchors.
Gear: 5 bolts   2-bolt anchor
FA: Alan Nelson 1998

192 Unknown O 5.11d ★

This is the narrow face between *Death of Innocents* and *Hate Hate*. Follow the bolts through powerful moves as the crack arcs right over the third bolt to join *Hate Hate* at the last bolt.
Gear: 5 bolts   shared anchor

193 Hate Hate 5.9+ ★

A dirty, juggy start with a tricky move leads into an obvious open book. Chimney up to a blocky overhang. Pull over it and fire to the anchors.
Gear: 4 bolts   2-bolt anchor
FA: Alan Nelson 1998

194 Unknown P 5.10a

Start 10ft left of the *Umph* dihedral. Climb a rounded arête and step right under a dirty, white-streaked roof. Undercling through the roof to positive holds and move up and left to the anchors on *Hate Hate*.
Gear: 4 bolts   shared anchor

195 Moment of Weakness 5.10b

Climb the narrow slab immediately left of *Umph*, making a balancy transition left at the third bolt. The name says it all.
Gear: 4 bolts   2-bolt anchor
FA: Dan Hare, Tom Kohlmann 2008

196 Umph 5.6 ★

Climb the chimney/open book immediately left of *D's Dry Dream* and rap from the ring anchors on that route.
Gear: SR   shared anchor

197 D's Dry Dream 5.10a ★★

Follow the bolt line on the left side of the arête shared with the following route. The line was intended to be climbed without using the back wall.
Gear: 7 bolts   2-bolt anchor

Laramie Duncan, *Mind Mantle Arete* (5.11a), p. 74

photo: Jason Haas

198 Lying on the Ground 5.11c ★★ ❑

This fun, steep, but one-move wonder of a route climbs the other side of the arête as for the previous route. Beware of z-clipping the retrobolted third bolt.
Gear: 4 bolts   2-bolt anchor
FA: Guy Lords, Ken Trout 1991

199 Don't Pout 'Cause Yer Down 'n Out (Fetus Smears) 5.8+ ❑

Climb the left-facing dihedral between *Lying on the Ground* and *Pigeon Pile Pinnacle*. Finish in the chimney formed between the main wall and the pinnacle, topping out above the following route.
Gear: SR   shared anchor

200 Pigeon Pile Pinnacle 5.10d ★ ❑

Blast up the right side of a detached pinnacle, powering through a crux at mid height. For extra credit, continue past the anchors and top out on the small summit. The original line climbed straight up the bolts, slightly left of where people climb now (5.11a).
Gear: 5 bolts   2-bolt anchor

201 Psychasthenia 5.12c ★★ ❑

This formerly abandoned project starts around the corner from *Pigeon Pile Pinnacle*. Clamber up to a headwall, crank through a distinct, deadpoint crux at two-thirds height, avoiding the stem off the pinnacle to the left.
Gear: 4 bolts   2-bolt anchor
FFA: Jason Haas 2008

202 The Plumber's Crack 5.10a ★ ❑

Climb *Intuition* past the initial corner to move left into an overhanging dihedral. Hang on through the leaning finish.
Gear: SR   2-bolt anchor
FA: Dan Hare, Cary Griner, Roland Fortin 2008

203 Intuition 5.7 ★ ❑

Begin in the back of a large, jumbled right-facing dihedral as for the last route. Climb up a broken dihedral to gain the first bolt, working up the rest of the skinny face to the top. A cam will reduce the runout between bolts.
Gear: 3 bolts   2-bolt anchor
FA: Pete Davis, Dan Hare 2008

204 Toast & Jam 5.7 ★ ❑

Move 20ft right of *Intuition* and climb a left-facing corner to a ledge 25ft up. Clip up the face, finishing with a perfect hand crack.
Gear: 2 bolts, SR   2-bolt anchor
FA: Dan Hare, Tom Kohlmann 2008

205 The Ground Doesn't Lie 5.10c ★ ❑

Start immediately right of *Toast & Jam* and climb up the center of the narrow face to the right of a large overhanging, left-facing dihedral.
Gear: 3 bolts   2-bolt anchor
FA: Ken Trout, Mike Carr, Rick Leitner 1990

Ben Schneider, *Mr. Squirrel Places a Nut* (5.11c), p.82   photo: Jason Haas

#224
#212
#264
Gully
South Quarry
1mi
ad
ly

**206 Top Rope Face
Two** 5.10b TR ★
Toprope the face to the right of the bolts
on the previous route using that anchor.

207 Beer Barrel Buttress 5.10d ★ ☐
Move 15ft right of the preceding route,
next to a deep gully system. Climb past
the first bolt to the top of a pedestal 12ft
up. Blast over a bulging headwall to a
slab finish.
Gear: 4 bolts   2-bolt anchor
FA: Dave Hart, Ernie Moskovics 1994

208 Sidelines 5.10a ★★ ☐
Begin 30ft right of *Beer Barrel Buttress*,
climbing up the face just right of a
blocky, right-facing dihedral to a
high first bolt 30ft up. Crimp up the
intimidating face, which is actually
easier than it looks.
Gear: 3 bolts   2-bolt anchor

**209 Beer Drinkers and
Hell Raisers** 5.8 ★ ☐
Climb the crack between the bolts on
Sidelines and the following route to a
tight v-slot. Continue up the crack until
it ends and finish on the face to gain the
anchors on *In Between the Lines*.
Gear: SR   shared anchors

210 In Between the Lines 5.9- ★ ☐
This squeeze job is the bolted line
between the previous route and the deep
Corniche crack/chimney.
Gear: 4 bolts   2-bolt anchor

211 Corniche 5.8 ★★ ☐
Climb a deep crack on the left side of
the narrow pillar for *Off Line*, utilizing
techniques ranging from chimneying to
face climbing. Rap from the anchors on
the previous route.
Gear: SR to #4 Camalot   shared anchor
FA: Scott and Richard Berk 1990

212 Off Line 5.8 ★★ ☐
This slender spinal column is 12ft left
of *Mr. Squirrel*. When the arête widens,
move up and right to the anchors.
Gear: 4 bolts   2-bolt anchor

81

North Quarry
← 1 mi

#85　#100　Access Fund
Property Line

Broad
Gully

#150

213 Mr. Squirrel Places a Nut
(Choreographed Revolution) 5.11c ★★★
This classic line graced the cover of a previous book. Climb a vertical face past four bolts to a large roof. Tackle it on the right side and enjoy easier moves above to the anchor. The difficulties below the roof can be cheated by climbing the crack system to the left.
Gear: 6 bolts　2-bolt anchor
FA: Ken Trout, Guy Lords, Mike Carr

214 Tora, Tora, Tora 5.11b ★★
Start 20ft right of *Mr. Squirrel* in a 5.8 gully with optional nut placements if desired. Gain a ledge 30ft up where the bolts and real climbing begins. Once on the ledge, climb the vertical face above on crisp edges to a pair of cold shuts. This is a great line if you don't factor in the start.
Gear: 3 bolts　2-bolt anchor
FA: Tod Anderson 1995
Variation: Begin to the left of the gully and follow three bolts directly up to the ledge and the upper half, eliminating the need for any trad gear.

215 Handle This Hard On
5.12a ★★★
This fun, technical line climbs the arête immediately right of the gully for *Tora, Tora, Tora*. A hard, thought provoking start eases up considerably at the third bolt. It is possible to set up a toprope for the crux by climbing up the gully on the left and reaching over to clip the bolt.
Gear: 5 bolts　2-bolt anchor

216 Toura Obscura 5.9 ★
Begin 10ft left of *Mrs. Hen Places a Peck* at a left-arcing bolt line on a rounded prow. Climb the right-facing dihedral just left of the bolt line and then move back over the left side of a large, flat roof. Follow several more bolts to the anchor.
Gear: 7 bolts　2-bolt anchor

217 Mr. Coors Contributes to the Pink Stain 5.9+ ★★★
This route climbs the crack through the double roofs to the left of *Here Today, Gone Tomorrow*. Use the anchor on the following route.
Gear: SR　shared anchor
FA: Scott and Richard Berk, Dave Hart 1987

218 Here Today, Gone Tomorrow 5.9 ★
Start up the previous route to gain a bolt on a detached, hanging arête 30ft up. Continue up the overhanging arête until the line moves up and left onto the upper headwall. The original line forced the arête at 5.11d avoiding the use of the good holds out left. It may be a good idea to bring a thin-hands cam for the start or longer draws to clip the first two bolts on the following route.
Gear: 5 bolts　2-bolt anchor
FA: Tod Anderson, Richard Wright

Scott Esser, *Tora, Tora, Tora* (5.11b), p. 82

photo: Jason Haas

219 Mrs. Hen Places a Peck (Revolution Butterfly) 5.11d ★★★

Start immediately right of the previous route and climb the slightly overhanging face along a seam to the anchors. Highly recommended as it is one of the steeper routes at Table.

Gear: 6 bolts   2-bolt anchor
FA: Chip Chase, Pat Adams 1990

Variation: Mr. Peery Takes a Bow 5.11b ★

Climb *Mrs. Hen* to the second bolt, then move up and left to climb the bolted arête of *Here Today, Gone Tomorrow*.

220 Chicken Dance 5.12a ★★

Begin immediately right of *Mrs. Hen* and climb past a distinct, volleyball-sized hueco just above the first bolt. Continue up the face above, moving back left after the last bolt to the anchors on *Mrs. Hen* before continuing on for another 10ft to a higher set of anchors. The original start began with the first few feet of *Hellraiser*, but a somewhat contrived direct start near the hueco was later bolted by another party.

Gear: 6 bolts   2-bolt anchor
FA: Dan Hare, Mo Hershoff 1999

221 Hellraiser 5.9 ★

Start immediately right of the previous route in a left-facing dihedral. Reach the top of a pillar and then continue up a deep crack that widens into a chimney. Belay on gear.

Gear: SR   nearby anchors

Variation: Toprope the narrow face to the right of the *Hellraiser* chimney, over a small overlap to a black face above.

222 Smear Me a Beer 5.11b ★

Start in a faint alcove with a narrow arête sticking out 15ft left of *This Ain't Naturita*. Climb past two bolts to a ledge before moving right to climb an arête that leads to chain anchors. The crux start may be avoided by chimneying the wall to the left at 5.8+.

Gear: 5 bolts   2-bolt anchor

223 Hellbound II 5.9+ ★★

Climb a deep open book that points slightly to the right and is between *Smear Me a Beer* and the following route. Reach a roof, bypassing it on the left in order to friction up to the anchors on the previous route.

Gear: SR   shared anchor

224 This Ain't Naturita Pilgrim 5.9 ★★★

This classic is coincidently located where the approach trail meets the main cliff, providing a great route with little searching. Balance up a blunt prow and over a two-foot roof at mid-height to the anchors.

Gear: 6 bolts   2-bolt anchor
FA: Ken Trout

North Quarry
← 1 mi

#85

#100

Access Fund
Property Line

Broad
Gully

#150

BROWN CLOUD CRAGS

Approach: Follow the approach trail uphill from the parking lot and continue past the Lower Child Free Zone to where the trail meets the main cliff at *This Ain't Naturita Pilgrim*. While there is no distinct break in the cliff separating Brown Cloud Crags from Overhang Area, the arbitrary break occurs here and all the routes to the right of this point are considered a part of Brown Cloud Crags. The area ends at a gully, which provides convenient access to the top of the cliff and the anchors for toproping.

225 Natural Fact 5.7 ★ ❑
Climb the obvious wide chimney, which forms the gap between the pillars for *This Ain't Naturita Pilgrim* and the following route. Slimmer climbers can tunnel under the large, wedged chockstone at the top, but most will prefer to climb out and around it. Rappel from the anchors on the following route.
Gear: SR   nearby anchor

226 The Fabulous Flying Carrs Route 5.11a ★★★ ❑
Begin next to a deep chockstone-filled chimney. Crimp past the bolt line to the anchors.
Gear: 5 bolts   2-bolt anchor
FA: Mike and Tom Carr

227 Another Unnamed Billy Bob Route (Sloping Forehead) 5.7 ★ ❑
Climb an arête five feet right of *Fabulous Flying Carrs Route*, transitioning right around to the other face and merging with *Pack O' Bobs* at the last bolt before the anchor just beyond the ledge.
Gear: 4 bolts   shared anchor

228 Pack O' Bobs 5.7 ★★★ ❑
(Ivory Tower)
This enjoyable warm-up starts on the other side of the arête as for the previous route and pulls over a difficult, overhanging start. From here, follow the face up and slightly left to an anchor just over a ledge.
Gear: 4 bolts   2-bolt anchor

229 Wholly Holey 5.8 ★ ❑
Move five feet right of *Pack O' Bobs* and locate a low first bolt on a slabby block seven feet up. Pull over a crux overhang at the second bolt and float up jugs to a ledge with chain anchors.
Gear: 6 bolts   2-bolt anchor
FA: Alan Nelson 2001

230 War with a Rack 5.8 ★ ❑
Begin eight feet right of *Wholly Holy* and jam over a slight bulge via a hand crack and into a right-facing dihedral. Continue up the corner and rappel from the anchor on *Wholly Holey*.
Gear: SR   nearby anchor

North Quarry
← 1 mi

#85 #100 ← Access Fund
Property Line

Broad Gully

#150

231 Iraqi Road 5.6 ☐

Climb the initial dihedral on the following route and then move left into a second bushy, right-facing corner. Top out and walk off to the right or use the anchors on *Brown Cloud Arête*.
Gear: SR   nearby anchor

232 Axis of Weasels 5.7 ★ ☐

Begin 10ft left of *Brown Cloud Arête* in a blocky, right-facing dihedral. Climb to the top of the dihedral and then continue straight up via a hand crack. Rap from anchors on *Brown Cloud Arête*.
Gear: SR   nearby anchor

233 Brown Cloud Arête 5.10a ★★★ ☐

This sport route climbs the pillar 40ft right of *Wholly Holy*, next to a deep, chockstone filled chimney. The difficult start can be cheated on the left.
Gear: 4 bolts   2-bolt anchor

234 Retro-Crack 5.9+ ★★ ☐

Climb the thin crack through the left side of a small overhang immediately left of *Pee on D* to the anchors on that route.
Gear: SR   shared-anchor

235 Pee on D 5.8 ★ ☐

Climb the slabby face, pulling over a small roof on the right.
Gear: 3 bolts   2-bolt anchor
Variation: Direct Start 5.10d ★★
Slap straight up the face without using the crack to the right or left to rejoin the original line higher up.

236 Windy Days 5.8 ★ ☐

Start just right of *Pee on D*, to the left of a large boulder forming a short, left-facing dihedral. Climb the slabby face.
Gear: 3 bolts   2-bolt anchor

237 Solo Route 5.11a ★ ☐

There is a 25ft tall boulder between *Windy Days* and the following route with a bolted toprope anchor on top. Get atop the boulder by scrambling up a left-facing dihedral near *Windy Days* or from scrambling down from on top of the cliff. Boulder up the seam-riddled face avoiding the left-hand arête to the top. First done as a boulder problem.

238 Punkin Puss & Mushmouse ☐
5.9+ ★★

Start immediately right of the preceding route at a short, bolted hand crack. Jam up to an arête and continue up to the anchors trying to avoid moving too far right from the arête towards *Deck Chairs*. Originally done on gear, bolts unknowingly added later by Ken Trout.
Gear: 7 bolts   2-bolt anchor
FA: Mike Cichon

239 Deck Chairs on the Titanic ☐
5.9+ ★★★

This sport route begins five feet right of the preceding route. Climb the deceptive face to the top with a crux start. Before bolts were added, it was known as *Rocky Mountain Acid Test*.
Gear: 6 bolts   2-bolt anchor
FA: Ken Trout, Rick Leitner 1991

240 Killian's Dead 5.6 ★★★ ☐

Begin five feet right of *Deck Chairs* in an open book, which changes to a right-facing dihedral after 12ft, and then changes again into a splitter hand crack after another 12ft just before the top.
Gear: SR   bolted anchor
FA: Richard Berk, Dave Hart 1987

#224
#212
Gully
#264
South Quarry
1mi →

236
237
238
239
240
241
242
243

241 John Adams' Adams Apple
5.7 ★
Start just right of *Killian's Dead* and climb a short face to a crack that widens from fingers to wide-hands. Top out and rappel from the anchors on *Killians Dead.*
Gear: SR   nearby anchor

242 Bullet the Brown Cloud
5.11b ★★★
Classic. Start 10ft right of the previous route on a west-facing arête. Climb a smooth arête to a ledge, utilizing both the face and arête. A few more face moves and another bolt leads to the anchors.
Gear: 4 bolts   2-bolt anchor
FA: K. Trout, Rick Leitner, Brian Kelligan 1992
Variation: 5.10c TR ★ Toprope the right side of arête.

243 Volobee 5.11b ★★★
Begin 15ft right and around the corner from *Bullet the Brown Cloud.* Scramble onto the top of a 20ft tall block to climb the clean, smooth face to a ledge with anchors.
Gear: 3 bolts   2-bolt anchor
FA: Mark Rolofson 1994

244 Tenacious 5.9+ ★★
(Surfing with the Aliens)
This often shaded east-facing route is 40ft right of *Volobee,* just before a deep gully/chimney. Climb the face over several ledges to a pair of cold shuts. It was intended to be climbed belly-to-the-bolts, avoiding the monster ledge out left.
Gear: 4 bolts   2-bolt anchor

#224
#212
Gully
#264
South Quarry
1mi

245 Left Slab (Interface) 5.8 ★

Move 15ft right of the preceding route to a nice, smooth slabby face that is 15ft right of a deep gully/chimney. Scramble up onto a 10ft tall boulder pile and climb a short face to a pair of rap hangers.
Gear: 4 bolts   2-bolt anchor
FA: Scott Berk solo 1988
Variation: 5.9 TR ★   Climb the slab further right of the bolt line.

246 Protection from the Virus
5.10c ★

Walk 80ft right of the previous route, past several short columns to a face and climb up the left side to a flat triangular roof above the first bolt. Awkwardly press under the roof, reach over for the jug and turn the lip and finish out the face. Also known as *Trident Submarines*.
Gear: 4 bolts   2-bolt anchor

247 Old Roof Route 5.8 ★★
(Lemons, Limes, and Tangerines)

Follow the face past the right side of a flat triangular roof to a large pedestal ledge. A few more balancy moves leads to the anchor.
Gear: 4 bolts   2-bolt anchor
FA: Dave Hart, T. Howard 1988

248 Big Dihedral 5.8 ★★★

This is the large, splitter left-facing dihedral immediately right of the previous route and is one of the best jam cracks at Table Mountain. Float up tight-hands that pinch down to an off-fingers layback over a small overlap, and then back to hands before reaching the anchor. Jugs conveniently appear whenever the crack pinches down.
Gear: SR   2-bolt anchor
FA: Scott and Richard Berk 1988

249 Rising Passion 5.10c ★
(Toprope Face Three)

This line is no longer just a toprope; bolts were added in 2004 by Dan Hare and Mo Hershoff. Start immediately right of *Big Dihedral* and scramble up to a high first bolt. Avoid the barn door while laybacking up the jug flake to gain the top.
Gear: 4 bolts   2-bolt anchor

Norie Kizaki, *Deck Chairs on the Titanic* (5.9+), p.88

photo: Jason Haas

#224
#212
Gully
#264
South Quarry
1mi →

250 **Thick Crust** 5.7 ★

This is the deep left-facing dihedral immediately left of *The Virus*. The first half is filled with avian deposits, however this nasty distraction can easily be avoided by grabbing holds closer to the front of the inset. Top out on a small pedestal and clip the anchors on the previous route.
Gear: SR   shared anchors

Brian Young, *The Virus* (5.12a)   photo: Ben Schneider

251 **The Virus** 5.12a ★★★

Start underneath a short table-top roof at head height and just below the first bolt. Engage a one-move wonder boulder problem past the first bolt. Casually saunter up the rest of the face and crack to the top.
Gear: 5 bolts   2-bolt anchor
Variation: 5.9- ★   Start in the dihedral to the left of the first bolt. Scamper up a few feet before traversing out right across a horizontal to merge with the regular line at the second bolt, thus skipping the crux.

247   248   250   251   252   253   254
toprope access

93

Jason Haas, *Bullet the Brown Cloud* (5.11b), p. 89

photo: Ben Schneider

#224
#212
Gully
#264
South Quarry
1mi
ad
lly

252 New River Gorge Homesick Blues 5.9+ ★★

Move 15ft right of *The Virus*. Climb up to the first bolt and then traverse hard left to a huge undercling. Punch it straight up to the anchors.

Gear: 4 bolts   2-bolt anchor
FA: Jonathon Houck, Jim Thilbodeau 1991

253 Kid's Climb 5.9 ★★ (Dave's Rave)

Start 10ft right of the previous route and climb a skinny pillar starting in a short, left-facing dihedral below the first bolt.

Gear: 4 bolts   2-bolt anchor
FA: Geoff and Tim Slater, Dillon Leitner

254 Thelma 5.7 ★

Begin on an arête 25ft right of *Kid's Climb*. Slap up the rounded prow to shared anchors with *Louise*. The route becomes easier the more one uses the right-facing corner to the left.

Gear: 3 bolts   shared anchor

255 Louise 5.8 ★

This short east-facing route is the last line on the wall and often sits in the shade, around the corner from the main cliff. Balance up the center of the face generously using the right hand arête.

Gear: 3 bolts   2-bolt anchor
Variation: 5.10a ★   This contrived variant avoids the juggy right-hand edge.

Broad
Gully

North Quarry
← 1 mi

#85   #100   Access Fund
Property Line

#150

UPPER CHILD FREE ZONE

Approach: The upper section is aptly named because it sits directly atop the lower section, where it is possible, though highly unlikely, for someone to walk off the top of the lower section and tumble down to the approach trail. A more likely scenario is for a climber at the Upper Child Free Zone to knock a rock down the hill onto climbers at the Lower Child Free Zone. Follow the approach trail uphill, passing the Lower Child Free Zone on the left side. 150ft beyond *Hair Ball* is another trail, which branches off uphill to the right from the main trail. Follow this diagonally up and right to a point just beyond a distinct gully that separates the Brown Cloud Crags from the Upper Child Free Zone.

256 Unknown Q 5.10b★   ☐

The trail to the upper zone reaches the main cliff at a gully separating Upper Child Free Zone from Brown Cloud Crags. Walk 100ft right of the gully to an alcove with two sport routes that share the first bolt. This route follows the left hand bolt line.

Gear: 5 bolts   2-bolt anchor

257 Big Loose Goose 5.10a ★   ☐

Climb to the first bolt on the previous route and then branch off to the right and climb alongside a right-hand arête to the top. The anchor is currently missing its hangers, which can be remedied by cinching a nut over the stud and traversing left to the anchor on the preceding route.

Gear: 6 bolts   2-bolt anchor

#224

#212

Gully

#264

South Quarry
1mi →

258 The Rodent 5.10a ★

Move 50ft right of the preceding route to a smooth wall near a left-facing dihedral. Begin on a pedestal with a bolt that can be reached from the ground and climb up either the right or left side of the face to the second bolt, where the route forces you towards the arête and a crack. Mantle onto a ledge and make a few more moves to gain the top.

Gear: 5 bolts   2-bolt anchor
FA: Dan Hare, Noel Childs 2004

259 Parental Abuse 5.11b ★★★

Hike 60ft right of *The Rodent* to the next sport route, which mostly contains red-painted cold shut hangers. Scamper up past a bolt and onto a ledge 15ft up. Crimp up the face, balance through a seam, catch the left-hand arête, and slap the top. Easier said than done.

Gear: 6 bolts   2-bolt anchor
FA: Mark Rolofson, Diane Dallin 1993

260 Mohare Eclaire 5.11c ★★★

Walk right of *Parental Abuse*, skirting over the top of a gully that breaks up the upper cliff band and find two bolted arêtes near the edge of a ledge system. This is the left of the two sport routes and begins at a two-bolt bottom belay anchor with painted black hangers. Climb into a short open book and mantle onto a ledge. Stay right of the arête, past a distinct crux, and follow easier but sustained moves to the top.

Gear: 8 bolts   2-bolt anchor
FA: Dan Hare, Mo Hershoff, Clair Mearns 2000

261 The Mohare Edge 5.12b ★★★

This is the better, harder counterpart to the preceding route. Gingerly work across the ledge system to the right of *Mohare Eclaire* and find a bottom two-bolt anchor for the belay. Clip up three easy bolts and then prepare to engage in some arête slapping, salsa dancing movement on the right side of the sustained arête to gain the anchor.

Gear: 9 bolts   two-bolt anchor
FA: Mo Hershoff, Dan Hare 1999

North Quarry
← 1 mi

#85   #100   ← Access Fund
Property Line

Broad
Gully

#150

LOWER CHILD FREE ZONE

Approach: The Child Free Zone, also known as the Parkway Crags, has an upper and lower section and makes up the far right side of the main area. The lower section is the first hunk of rock that is reached when walking up the approach trail from the main parking lot and is 100ft below the main rock wall. Routes at the lower zone are listed from left to right.

262 Hair Ball V0- R ★ ❑

Hike up the trail past the main bolted routes of the Lower Child Free Zone, which lie 100ft to the right. There is a short but prominent pillar with good flat jugs on it just before the cliff breaks down and the trail continues up to the main wall. Boulder up the prow and top out, scrambling back down to the right.

263 Puzzled Monkey 5.11a ★ ❑

Identify a prominent pillar with a three-foot roof going through the center of it on the tallest section of the lower cliff band. Climb the bolt line on the left side of the prow, stemming up the gentle overhang to stay in line with the first few bolts instead cheating around to the face on the left. Going straight up provides better movement and allows for a more consistently difficult route.
Gear: 4 bolts   2-bolt anchor
FA: Tod Anderson, Richard Wright 1996

264 Monkey Puzzle 5.12a ★★★ ❑

Begin immediately right of *Puzzled Monkey* and climb directly up the center of the prow to a large roof. Mellow climbing leads to a definitive V4 boulder problem that can be more readily solved with cunning technique rather than simple brute force.
Gear: 6 bolts   2-bolt anchor

265 Rafiki 5.12c ★ ❑

Find this bolted line a few feet left of a wide offwidth on the right side of the Monkey Pillar. Climb up the face using the crack for help with the right hand while slapping up the rounded prow with the left hand. The route moves away from the crack at the third bolt to face the first crux. Power and balance gains the fourth bolt and another crux with a fun dead point. A nice rest and a casual roof lead to the anchors.
Gear: 6 bolts   2-bolt anchor
FA: Mark Tarrant, Greg Purnell, R.Wright 2003

266 Power and Lies 5.10a ★ ❑

Move 15ft right of *Rafiki* to the other side of a small alcove. While the original intention was to climb the arête head on, most people will opt for the shallow corner to the left of the bolt line. Top out on a ledge near the anchors of *Off Guard* and continue up another 15ft to a higher set of chains.
Gear: 8 bolts   2-bolt anchor
FA: R. Wright, M. Tarrant, Lisa Veraldi 2003
Variation: 5.7 ★   Climb just the crack to the left of the bolt line.

267 Off Guard 5.10a ★★ ❑

Climb the prow to a left-hand arête just right of *Power and Lies*. Mantle onto a sloping ledge and gain the anchors.
Gear: 6 bolts   2-bolt anchor
FA: Richard Wright, Lisa Veraldi 2003

#224

#212

Gully

#264

South Quarry
1mi →

259

263 264 265 266 267 268

262

268 **Cool Thing** 5.11a ★ ☐
Start just right of *Off Guard* and climb
up the easy face to an awkward layback.
Pull onto a ramped ledge to reach
anchors shared with *Off Guard*.
Gear: 6 bolts   shared anchor
FA: Richard Wright, M. Tarrant, L. Veraldi 2003

269 **Fergus Traverse** V1 ★★ ☐
Begin just left of the following route and
traverse rightward across the base of the
wall to a point just beyond *Skin Deep*.
The traverse alternates between good
holds with bad feet to bad holds with
good feet and back again.

99

Tony Bubb, *Monkey Puzzle* (5.12a), p.98

#224
#212
Gully
#264
South Quarry
1mi →

271 **Skin Deep** 5.10a ★

Begin 40ft right of *Uommama bin Rotten* at the right-most bolted route on the crag, just before the cliff breaks down and curves around into a valley. Scamper onto a ledge at chest height before tackling a short, bouldery crux. The upper third of the route is currently a little flakey, but should clean up with time.

Gear: 6 bolts   2-bolt anchor
FA: Richard Wright, Anna Brandenburg-Schroeder 1998

270 **Uommama bin Rotten** 5.10b X

This is the worst route at Table; do not climb it. Walk 300ft right of *Cool Thing* past a rotten section of cliff with several gullies leading up to the Upper Child Free Zone to a point 40ft left of the bolts on the following route. Climb a gray left-facing corner system being very careful of loose rock (there's a lot of it). Sift through a low-angled choss band of consolidated mud to gain the higher section. Follow a crack to the side of a chimney to gain the anchor. **60m rope.**

Gear: SR   3-bolt anchor
FA: Alan Nelson

Louie Russo, *Henry Spies the Line* (5.10a), p. 76

101

John Langston, *Bone Crusher* (5.12b), p. 104   photo: Ben Schneider

SOUTH QUARRY

This wall is easily seen from CO-58 and is the large white area just left of the power lines. It was largely overlooked for years because of its isolation from the main crag, but also because from far away, the rock looks chossy. Wayne Crill and friends went up in the winter of 2004/2005 and discovered quite the opposite. Splitter cracks through bomber rock, uncharacteristic of most of the cliff at Table, provided instant classic test-pieces.

Approach: From Washington Ave, head east on 10th St. for 1.6mi. Drive under the highway and then turn left onto Easley Rd. Follow the S-curve for 0.1mi to a stop sign and park at a dirt pull off on the right. If you turned left, you would get back onto the highway via an on ramp. Hike up the road along the on ramp to a point just beyond the last house, near the power lines. Follow a climber's trail up along the gravely, tiered rock band which often has classes from the School of Mines poking around. Another five minutes up the hill leads to the main cliff a bit left of the large power lines.

North Quarry
← 1 mi
#85   #100   ← Access Fund
Property Line
#150
Broad Gully

272 **Frank's Wild Years** 5.11c ★★★ ❏

Begin around the corner to the left of
Silver Bullet. Climb up the crack, making
a hand traverse left halfway up. Follow
the crack and corner system to the top.
Gear: SR   2-bolt anchor
FA: Hank Caylor

273 **Silver Bullet** 5.11d ★★★ ❏

This is another classic trad route and
is the middle of the three cracks on the
buttress. Sustained jamming with a few
cruxes leads to the anchor.
Gear: SR   2-bolt anchor
FA: Wayne Crill

274 **Bone Crusher** 5.12b ★★★ ❏

Begin just right of *Silver Bullet.* This
beautiful crack is the best trad line at
Table Mountain and a quality route for
any area in Colorado. Follow sustained
jamming up the right side of the bulging
headwall.
Gear: SR   2-bolt anchor
FA: Jimmy Menendez

275 **Hank's Project** ❏

Move 200ft right of *Bone Crusher* to a
seam going through red rock. Climb up
the seam to two fixed nuts and continue
up the unprotected slab above to No
Man's Land. Currently, no anchor exists.
Expect hard, scary climbing.
Gear: SR   NO anchor

276 **Marry Me Becky** 5.10c ★★ ❏

Walk 250ft right of *Bone Crusher* to the
left side of the main buttress and climb
crack systems up to a ledge. Finish in the
overhanging offwidth crack. Too bad it
isn't longer or more sustained.
Gear: SR to #4.5 Camalot   2-bolt anchor
FA: Kevin Gallagher

#224
#212
Gully
#264
South Quarry
1mi

277 The Crill-Menendez
5.12c TR ★★
Jam and stem a funky crack in an open book five feet left of *The Short Tour*. Delicately pull on thin flakes under the roof to a good edge on the lip. Battle it out to the top. The bolted anchor is easily accessed from the *Short Tour* anchors.

278 The Short Tour 5.9 ★★★
This quality hand crack offers more jamming than the typical Table route.
Gear: SR   2-bolt anchor
FA: Wayne Crill

279 The Bowels 5.8- ★
This offwidth begins just right of the previous route and is marked by a large flake propped inside an even larger crack. Awkward moves around this flake lead to solid hands through a small roof. Beware of some loose blocks and use the anchors on *Short Tour*.
Gear: SR to #5 Camalot   shared anchor
FA: Wayne Crill

280 Offwidth Bulge 5.9 ★
This extended boulder problem starts a few feet right of *The Bowels*.
Gear: SR to #5 Camalot   walk off
FA: Wayne Crill

281 Warm-Up Crack 5.8 ★
When hiking up to the main area, this extended boulder problem consisting of splitter hands will be the first route encountered. Worth doing if in the area.
Gear: SR   walk off
FA: Wayne Crill

282 Something To Do V0 ★
Right above the quarry where the approach trail reaches the rock near *Warm-Up Crack* is a boulder with a flat, vertical east face. Start near a hand crack and move up and left on flat edges to the top.

283 The Whale V3 ★★★
From *Something To Do*, walk around to the opposite side of the boulder. Sit start at a flat jug and then slap up side pulls to a sloper top out. The less graceful may beach whale the finish.

284 Finger Wrecker V2 ★
Directly behind *The Crill Menendez* and in front of *The Whale* boulder is a short, wide block with a perfect finger crack splitting the center of it. A hard start with perfect locks and terrible feet quickly lets up to easier moves above.

SPORT ROUTE INDEX

TRAD ROUTE INDEX

BOULDERING INDEX

ALPHABETICAL INDEX

ADVERTISERS

Craig Weinhold, *Heidi Hi* (5.8), p. 58   photo: Jason Haas

Mike Bronson, *Major Bolt Achievement* (5.11a), p.66　　　　photo: Kate Calde

North Table Mountain,
    Golden Colorado

Arkansas' first comprehensive, color guidebook written by loca
Cole Fennel includes nearly 1,300 routes at: Horseshoe Canyon
Ranch, Sam's Throne, Stack Rock, Cave Creek, Mt. Magazine,
Lincoln Lake, Haw Creek, Valley of the Blind, Shepard Springs,
Deliverance, and Rickett's/Owens. Also includes over 300 boulc
problems to Horsehoe Canyon Ranch and other areas!
Due out Fall 2009.

ABOUT THE AUTHORS
(we lovingly chose each other's photo and wrote these bios for one another)

JASON HAAS

This is Jason's second book, also authoring *Boulder's Flatirons: A Climber's Guide.* He teaches high school special education in Thornton, CO, and, as shown in the picture to the left, has always been easily upset when he can't go climbing. However, because Jason has always been a bit of a punk and because of his love for choss and obscure routes and crags (North Table Mountain being the obvious exception), it's not hard to see why his steady partners are few and far between. Whenever anyone is listening to him (this is usually just his students because they have no choice), Jason professes a true love of soloing; the truth about his love life, however, is that he has an unusually strong attachment to his dog Trango.

BEN SCHNEIDER

Ben migrated from Denver to Boulder just before the beginning of his high school years. He is a proud graduate of New Vista High School, but unlike many of his classmates has been unable to extricate himself from *the republic.* Ben enjoys giving back to the community in which he is a high school teacher, Thornton, CO. Yes, Ben and Jason both have day jobs teaching together. Ben experiences carbon-guilt and has sought to justify his inability to leave Boulder while teaching in Denver by driving a Honda Civic and a motorcycle, showing the duality of his personality.

Dan Dalton, *Big Dihedral* (5.8), p. 91